Praise for *Demanding More*

Many in the dominant majority have a hard time understanding how their privilege shows up in the workplace. In *Demanding More*, Sheree Atcheson has done a great job of peeling back the layers and offering tangible solutions to make the workplace more equitable.

Demanding More is a great read for anyone interested in understanding how to create true inclusion and dismantle the barriers faced by many. The book tackles key topics including privilege, intersectionality and how to be an ally, all of which are critical to understand in order to make real progress. Sheree Atcheson brings together great examples and experiences that captivate you to want to read more and more.

Demanding More is the result of almost a decade of impactful work and rework carried out by Sheree Atcheson. It is necessary reading for anyone who is alive in the 21st century and working or considering working. Even more so as we continue to develop what will be the future of work. Deep theory very quickly turns to tangible actions for everyone to perform and become better at, with the result of a fairer society and better realization of human potential. I'm so thankful Sheree Atcheson has put this together. I'll certainly be making it mandatory reading at organizations I work with.

D0220750

Diversity has rapidly become an issue that no company, organization or person can ignore, with expectations and demands to go beyond performative and shallow commitments. In *Demanding More*, Sheree Atcheson explains clearly what diversity and inclusion are and why they matter and offers concrete ways to achieve change in workplaces and beyond. It's an excellent book for anyone who is committed to genuinely move towards a more diverse society.

BEATRICE FIHN, EXECUTIVE DIRECTOR, INTERNATIONAL CAMPAIGN TO ABOLISH NUCLEAR WEAPONS, NOBEL PEACE PRIZE 2017

If you read one book on diversity and inclusion this year, *Demanding More* is the one. Sheree Atcheson has lived, breathed and worn the D&I t-shirt for many years, and her insights into why we're still falling short are invaluable. This book will have you take a deeper look at yourself, your privilege and your potential to be a greater ally and leader. Go read it now!

ANN O'DEA, CEO AND CO-FOUNDER, SILICON REPUBLIC, AND CURATOR, FUTURE HUMAN

Sheree Atcheson brings her rich personal and professional life, both lived and experienced, using the many frictions in the journey of a young professional woman of colour to bear on one of the most vexing global issues of today: exclusion and racial injustice. In *Demanding More*, a timely and urgent call to action, Atcheson makes a compelling case on moving diversity and inclusion from a 'nice to have' and strive-towards target, to a must-have imperative and achievable goal, while showing how to translate good intent and words into meaningful action and lasting change.

RAJU NARISETTI, FOUNDER, MINT (WWW.LIVEMINT.COM), AND FORMER MANAGING EDITOR, *THE WASHINGTON POST* AND *THE WALL STREET JOURNAL*

Being an ally is a journey, and Sheree Atcheson's powerful new book is the perfect accompaniment. In *Demanding More*, you'll be inspired by Atcheson and her extensive interviews with leaders to take stock of your privilege and use it for good.

KAREN CATLIN, AUTHOR OF *BETTER ALLIES*

A thought-provoking, incredibly well-researched and comprehensive overview of how diversity, equity and inclusion manifest in society – and particularly the workplace – today. *Demanding More* offers both clear explanations of complicated issues as well as practical advice on what can be done to drive change. A powerful guide for those starting out as well as for those more experienced in the space.

AMALI DE ALWIS, MD, MICROSOFT FOR STARTUPS UK, AND FORMER CEO, CODE FIRST: GIRLS

At a time when all leaders should be doing more to embrace and accelerate change in the workplace, *Demanding More* is a highly recommended read! It is a helpful resource that will inspire you to have those all-important difficult conversations that we all need to have in order to combat inequality and make the world a better place. Sheree Atcheson takes us on a transparent personal and professional journey, drawing on some great examples, practical exercises and recommendations from a range of progressive leaders. This book not only highlights some of the systemic reasons for inequalities in society but offers a road map for how we can demand actionable change from leaders and build more equitable workplaces.

PRISCILLA BAFFOUR, GLOBAL HEAD OF DIVERSITY AND INCLUSION, *FINANCIAL TIMES*

Demanding More is THE diversity and inclusion book we all need right now. It paints a very clear picture of the structural bias we see every day, with new and interesting meaningful ways to change the trajectory we are currently on. We need to have more personal accountability to lead to systemic and long-term change and this book helps with just that. I would recommend it to anyone, at any stage of their career, who wants to understand more about why we're at where we are and how to get us to a better place.

DEEPA PURUSHOTHAMAN, LEADER IN PRACTICE, WOMEN AND PUBLIC POLICY PROGRAM, HARVARD KENNEDY SCHOOL

Whether you are new to the concepts of diversity, inclusion and belonging or have worked with them for years, *Demanding More* is an invaluable resource for understanding both the theory and practical steps we can all take to change not just our workplace, but ourselves. Sheree Atcheson helps us consider inclusion in its fullest sense and how to become allies, whatever our role or status. Her discussions on privilege and intersectionality are amongst the best I've seen. Each chapter is clear and insightful about the problems but then moves to solutions and gives the reader practical steps to effect change. This is a book that brings together history, theory, practicality and deeply human voices to give us a road map to demand more of our managers, our leaders and, most importantly, ourselves. Highly recommended.

DEBBIE FORSTER MBE, CEO, TECH TALENT CHARTER

Demanding More covers the fundamentals with absolute clarity and straightforwardness. The combination of history, data, personal perspective and fascinating interviews with leaders makes this an utterly compelling piece of writing. If you are a leader, or an aspiring leader, who wants to understand more and do better, read this book and go away equipped with meaningful insights and practical guidance, galvanized to do more.

RUTH YARNIT, CEO, LEADDEV

Sheree Atcheson's book couldn't have come at a better time, as everyone is struggling not only to understand the issues around inclusion and diversity but also to move beyond words to the actions that drive long-term sustainable change. It is written in a style that is easy to read and relate to and will provide valuable insights for leaders, practitioners and individuals. I'm adding it to my recommended reading list!

BRENDA TRENOWDEN CBE, FORMER GLOBAL CHAIR, 30% CLUB, AND PWC LEAD PARTNER, I&D CONSULTING

Sheree Atcheson has leveraged her years of work as a practitioner for transformation by writing this manuscript that speaks 'truth to power' in *Demanding More*. We are all faced with the fierce urgency of now, and *Demanding More* is a blueprint that every leader who truly aspires to be more inclusive should have and apply. Every organization that really wants to move the needle of equity should make reading *Demanding More* a leadership development requirement. This is so powerful because it takes the real workplace challenges of intersectionality, privilege, authentic allyship and inclusion and meets the reader at the juncture of theory and application, so you walk away not only inspired, but also ready for implementation. I would recommend this book for anyone and everyone who feels a calling to make a difference and be a part of the solution.

DR JOHNÉ BATTLE, VICE PRESIDENT OF DIVERSITY AND INCLUSION, DOLLAR GENERAL

Sheree Atcheson has called on her hard-won experience as a woman of colour in the tech industry to craft an urgently relevant debut book that makes the case for why everyone should – and must – demand more from our leaders. *Demanding More*'s impressive range applies a personal and systemic lens to everything from equity and intersectionality, to privilege and authentic allyship. Readers from all fields will find insight in powerful real-world stories, all filtered through Sheree Atcheson's refreshing voice as a promising author.

JENNIFER BROWN, FOUNDER AND CEO, JENNIFER BROWN CONSULTING, AND AUTHOR OF *HOW TO BE AN INCLUSIVE LEADER*

Demanding More is exactly what we need right now as a collective society. We must move past awareness, with less talk and more action. Sheree Atcheson's book does just that through providing real-world, data-driven, meaningful insights to educate us all on why we're in the position we are right now and what we can do singularly and collectively to push for real, sustainable, meaningful change. This book is relevant to absolutely anyone who wants to leave the world better than they found it. Don't miss this one!

DEANNA SINGH, CHIEF CHANGE AGENT, FLYING ELEPHANT, FOUNDER, UPLIFTING IMPACT, AND AUTHOR OF *PURPOSEFUL HUSTLE*

Demanding More is exactly what we need. Sheree Atcheson does not shy away from a difficult subject and makes it clear that people need to be comfortable with the uncomfortable. Atcheson is brave, courageous and unapologetic! I could not be more excited for people to read and feel inspired to put her words into practice.

MICHELLE GROVER, CHIEF INFORMATION OFFICER, TWILIO, AND FORMER SENIOR VICE PRESIDENT OF ENGINEERING, CONCUR/SAP

Demanding More

Why diversity and inclusion don't happen
and what you can do about it

Sheree Atcheson

KoganPage

First published in Great Britain and the United States in 2021 by Kogan Page Limited

Apart from any fair dealing for the purposes of research or private study, or criticism or review, as permitted under the Copyright, Designs and Patents Act 1988, this publication may only be reproduced, stored or transmitted, in any form or by any means, with the prior permission in writing of the publishers, or in the case of reprographic reproduction in accordance with the terms and licences issued by the CLA. Enquiries concerning reproduction outside these terms should be sent to the publishers at the undermentioned addresses:

2nd Floor, 45 Gee Street	122 W 27th St, 10th Floor	4737/23 Ansari Road
London	New York, NY 10001	Daryaganj
EC1V 3RS	USA	New Delhi 110002
United Kingdom		India

www.koganpage.com

Kogan Page books are printed on paper from sustainable forests.

ISBNs

Hardback   978 1 3986 0054 6
Paperback   978 1 3986 0044 7
eBook   978 1 3986 0053 9

British Library Cataloguing-in-Publication Data

A CIP record for this book is available from the British Library.

Library of Congress Cataloging-in-Publication Data is available.

Control Number: 2021001339

Typeset by Integra Software Services, Pondicherry
Print production managed by Jellyfish
Printed and bound by CPI Group (UK) Ltd, Croydon CR0 4YY

Contents

Foreword

By Alaina Percival, CEO, Women Who Code

Insight is a rare thing. It requires an understanding that goes beyond the surface and comprehends the depths of a problem in a personal way. In this book, you will be given access to insight through the eyes of someone who has seen the world through many different lenses and who has something powerful to say.

Sheree was always going to make an impact on the world. She has an inner strength that allows her to push past boundaries and achieve near-impossible things. This is coupled with an authenticity that allows her message to connect with people.

I met Sheree for the first time when she reached out about expanding Women Who Code to the United Kingdom. She was recently out of university, but it was already clear that she understood the importance of our mission and had a vision for how it could have a positive impact on the communities around her. After several discussions she led the Women Who Code expansion to Belfast.

The network in Belfast was an incredible success and she soon identified leaders and replicated the growth in Bristol, London and later Edinburgh and Dublin. Her drive and her passion helped us to connect with people and build new communities. And it wasn't just the launches. She was there to lead those communities to grow until they were thriving on their own.

She had become a leader. She was giving talks, she was leading events, and the industry started recognizing that. They saw that same incredible spark that I did, and she started getting opportunities to participate in larger industry-wide events and even develop her own.

I had the opportunity to join Sheree on the stage at Belfast Technology Conference in 2014. She was only in her early twenties, but she had the ear of executives and politicians and had started to garner media attention.

On that same trip we had the opportunity to help give away the IET IngeNIous Female Student Award and deliver a round table discussion to tech leaders at the US Consulate General in Belfast. I remember thinking how remarkable it was that she had been able to gain access to the Lord Mayor and the C-suite to make all of this possible.

My second opportunity to meet her in person and to see her speak in person was at a talk series put on by Women Who Code at Yelp's offices in San Francisco. I was inspired by her ability to be authentic in a meaningful way. When she spoke, you could tell that there was truth and passion behind her words.

Since the early years, she has become an international thought leader for diversity, equity and inclusion in technology. She has shared her expertise across the globe and continues to use her voice, not only to increase access for people at her place of work, but also to change the face of the industry.

This book is more important now than ever, because the world is going through a crisis, and crisis creates an opportunity for change. We have an opportunity to peel back the layers of exclusion and take a real look at how economy, society and community work. We can see what has to be done if we only look. And Sheree provides insight that is invaluable in that quest.

Right now, people and industry are starting to buy into that change. They truly want to evolve and grow. But what is clear is that most companies don't know the steps that are needed to bring about that change internally, intentionally and organizationally.

Sheree has experienced both discrimination and privilege, and from that she has learned the compassion to help us all expand our world view. She takes the lessons from her lived experience and from that of those she's connected with, and distils them down into practical advice that can help us be better employers, co-workers, family and friends.

In this book she distils the wisdom of those experiences into a conversation that we all can have with ourselves about the nature of privilege and the way that it factors into our lives. By understanding that in ourselves, we can better understand the people around us and have compounding empathy for their perspectives.

To my amazing partner Sean – thank you for always having my back, never letting me give up even when I want to and being my best friend through everything that life has thrown at us. And of course, to Alfie for being the glue that holds our little family together.

To my brother David – thank you for always being the best little yet big brother I could ever have wanted, even if I do annoy you most of the time.

And finally, to my Dad – thank you for being my Dad, teaching me that I can do whatever I want to if I put my mind to it and that boundaries are simply there to be broken.

CHAPTER ONE

Sheree's story

This chapter will focus on:

- Who I am
- My personal story and journey
- Why I do what I do

Let's start from the beginning.

Who I am

I'm Sheree Atcheson. I'm a multi-award-winning diversity and inclusion leader. We will get to what that actually means in a little bit, but I want to share my story and explain how I've got to where I am now.

I am of Sri Lankan origin, and I was adopted, along with my brother (whom I am not biologically related to), at three weeks old by George and Marian Atcheson, an Irish couple living in Co. Tyrone. My parents were married in their early twenties and both grew up in typical Catholic families – the father goes to work and the mother works by maintaining the household and looking after the children. My dad is one of three boys and my mother is one of seven – six girls and one boy. They settled outside Coalisland, a town known for previously being a centre for … you guessed it … coal mines.

Unfortunately, or fortunately, my parents could not have children. I say 'unfortunately or fortunately' because it is a horrible, life-changing experience for a couple to go through, no less back in a time when support was much less readily available. Because of this, however, I have had the privilege of being here and in the grand scheme of things, my brother and I are incredibly lucky to have been adopted.

My family was not wealthy but my parents worked incredibly hard to make sure that at Christmas there was always an overload of gifts. It's not lost on me now that this meant various sacrifices throughout the year for this moment on that one day. Neither of my parents went to university, although my mother later went back to school to become a psychotherapist. But back then, most families from a working-class background went straight into work. There were lots of factories and lots of labour work. My mother worked as a seamstress in Coalisland's shirt factory and my dad worked as a welder. It's impossible to talk about our parents being raised in Ireland to not talk about the divide or the differences in upbringings that gives us.

You might wonder why the personal story of an adopted little girl of colour in Co. Tyrone is important. It is important because it is ultimately an example of being underrepresented yet privileged. Personally, my story is incredibly layered and nuanced with many elements of clear privilege, but it is also laced with different areas of exclusion and underrepresentation. I still very much live that life, despite my privilege of leadership and financial stability evolving.

My parents met at a 'dance' during the time of the civil war (or 'The Troubles'). I remember them telling us stories of how they used to go out to dances and hear soldiers shouting to get down as tracer bullets would go off above their heads.

They got married, moved to Co. Tyrone and decided to start their own family. This firstly came in the form of Patch, their Springer Spaniel. I mention Patch because he was my best friend. Any chapter about my background can't ignore or leave him out.

After many failed attempts at having children, a nurse looking after my mother mentioned a relative of theirs adopting a child from Sri Lanka. And that kicked off the idea for my parents.

There is a lot of discussion around white people adopting children from other countries as opposed to adopting from their own countries. In general, the focus of the debate is around whether or not that constitutes what is called 'white saviourism', which is when white people provide help or support to non-white people in a self-serving manner. This discussion has really been given weight in the 2010s, with groups like No White Saviours sharing things that we all need to hear. This is important because, for me, this shapes how I see the world, how the world has seen and treated me and how it feeds into the work I do every day. It's important to self-reflect and assess the actions of the people around us. What might be viewed as generosity or well-meaning charity work can in fact be steeped in colonialism and racism, if you scratch the surface. Intention and impact are two different things.

White saviourism is something I think about a lot, as an adopted child of colour into a very white space. There is no doubt that I am very privileged to have had the opportunities my adoption has given me, but there is a very real conversation around how many white adoptive parents or people have used this as a way to laud themselves above Black and brown people. You may have heard of Renee Bach. As reported in *The New Yorker*, Renee Bach is a white woman missionary who believed that her 'calling' was to go to Uganda to 'help people'. 'Not a doctor but a homeschooled missionary', she ran a facility taking in sick and malnourished children (Levy, 2020). It has been reported that in her care, over 105 Black Ugandan children died and a number of families have come forward accusing her of medical malpractice and seeking criminal prosecution. Though not a medical professional, a gardener that worked for her reported that she walked around wearing a stethoscope, very much giving the impression she was a medical professional, and she was reported to perform a number of medical procedures on the children, including blood transfusions (Mwesigwa and Beaumont, 2019). The lawsuit, which was brought by two women, has now been settled out of court (Aizenman, 2020). What is notable is that she is from an area in the United States that also includes poor families from low economic backgrounds, yet she felt her 'calling' was to help people in another country. Take pause and consider if she would have been allowed to practise and involve herself in medical procedures as an untrained missionary had she stayed in the United States.

Being honest, I have sat down and considered whether white saviourism played a role in my adoption. There is an obvious difference in severity in white missionary work with someone that performs unauthorized medical procedures and someone adopting a Black or brown baby (if you look after the child well). There are many conflicting and differing opinions on this, but it is still something I consider. I can't be 100 per cent sure. Does it matter who adopts a child if they want to give them a loving, caring home? Should a child only be placed with parents of similar ethnicities or is it ok for parents to be of different ethnicities if they are aware of the nuance around transracial adoptions? Honestly, I can't answer that.

My parents spent lots of time out in Sri Lanka finding the local community leaders and school teachers that needed supplies and money, and providing that to them. There were no photos, no showcasing of efforts, nor should there have been. They also actively tried to support our biological parents by sharing the small expendable income they had. There is always the question about whether they should have adopted a white child instead of myself and my brother, but on a personal level, I am greatly appreciative of what my parents have done for me, even though it hasn't always been easy.

My brother David and I are both dark-skinned. I say this because it's important. To put this into context, Northern Ireland's population according to the last census data is 2 per cent Black, Asian or people from ethnic minorities (Wikipedia, 2020). Where we grew up, there were not many people like us, and there certainly weren't many children like us. Most children looked like their parents and therefore avoided altogether the usual questions we would get routinely, like 'where did you come from?', 'where are you *really from*?', or the outright dismay that we would call our parents 'Mum' and 'Dad' despite the fact they were raising us. My brother is notably darker than I am and colourism has very clearly played into our differing experiences as we have got older. We will chat about colourism later in Chapter 4 on intersectionality.

People don't talk about racism because it makes them uncomfortable. It makes people even more uncomfortable to talk about racism when it's about people they know perpetuating it. Growing up in Ireland was a privilege, but it didn't come without its fair share of difficulties. We went to an amazing primary school and had some great friends there, some of whom my brother and I are still in contact with. When we were old enough to understand (around four or five), my parents explained openly how we were adopted, why and what it meant to them. We always knew we were adopted – how can you hide it when both white parents (who haven't had kids with previous partners) have two dark-skinned babies. In primary school, we never noticed any difference. I remember notably drawing a picture of me and my friends in school and colouring us all in pink, bringing the picture home and my parents asking me which one was me, and me pointing to one of the pink-coloured people.

Things change when you get older though. You are no longer the cute brown baby with a nice story. You're then just someone who is glaringly different from everyone else around you. My middle name is Nirushika and I was almost called Nirushika Atcheson. I think regularly about how much privilege is in a name and how the world would be different to me if I had a Sri Lankan name and accent. My brother and I started to experience racism more so when we were in our early teens – walking from school into the town and getting called monkeys, or the n-word, people making fun of my name calling me 'Sheree Lanka' or regularly being the butt of the joke because of my dark skin and small frame.

Because of this, I threw myself into my studies, and that's where I found my love of coding. I had a phenomenal teacher called Mr Owen Gribbin. He was so passionate about computing and anyone who had the privilege of being taught by him felt that. It was glaringly obvious he could have made a substantial impact in industry through himself singularly, but he dedicated himself to passing on his knowledge and interests to the next generation, who would then go on and make that impact. From the age of 11, I knew I wanted to be in technology. I created my own websites on my dogs, and I was enthralled by how I could create something new, instead of just using the solutions someone else made. I passed all my A Levels with A's and went to Queen's University in Belfast to study computer science.

Why I do what I do

Until university, I had never really been around people of lots of different ethnicities. Where I grew up was overwhelmingly white, as you'd expect. However, Belfast was different. It was still mostly white, but there was a notable change in the different kinds of people I saw day to day and in my university classes. This was different to me. I still stood out, but not as much as before! One of the things that was obvious though was the lack of women on my course. Out of 100 people, there were 10 women, including myself. From there, I started to get interested in why that was and what I could do to help change that. It is difficult being the only person like you, walking into a room where there are few people like you. It's not something that's easily done but you do get used to it.

The same gender disparity was clear when I became a software engineer, with a very small number of women being at the company I joined. I was ok with it, but I also didn't understand it – and it didn't feel very fair. So, I wanted to try to do something to make it better.

I wanted to create something that brought together women from all backgrounds, regardless of where they worked and help them get into and stay in an industry they loved – for free. This was really important to me; not everyone can afford £5, £10 or £15 on a meetup and I refused to create another element of exclusion. That's when I found Women Who Code.

At that stage, Women Who Code was a group, predominantly focused in the United States, providing free monthly meetups on technical skills to their approximately 5,000 members. For me, this was it. A group that had a strong branding and helped bridge the gap between knowledge access and a sense of community and belonging. To kick off the Women Who Code UK expansion, I launched in Belfast. The community in Belfast was phenomenally supportive, from tech specialists offering their time for sessions to companies lining up to host us. I built up an amazing remote team of women from all different backgrounds and had the privilege of watching so many women come together and find a real sense of belonging and 'one-ness'. It wasn't always easy. I was 22, doing all this work whilst also holding down a software engineer role. During this launch, I began to get a lot of requests from mainland UK to launch branches there – so I launched branches in London and Bristol, then helped kick off branches in Edinburgh and in other places across Europe. During these years, I was entirely focused on building teams, then stepping back and allowing them to grow and flourish without me. I was always there for help and advice, but this was not my journey – it was theirs.

Whilst I was launching branches, I was spending a lot of time helping organizations with their diversity and inclusion strategies, firstly through creating partnerships with Women Who Code and then actively working with them on tailored inclusion strategies.

It became really clear to me that this was what I wanted to do as my full-time job. I was excited and passionate about it.

At this stage, I was writing for the *HuffPost* and speaking at conferences globally. People like me do not normally do things like this. Young women of colour from lower socioeconomic backgrounds were and are regularly sidelined or discounted before they even start. There is a known 'double-bind' for women of colour – to not be too successful so as not to overpower anyone else but also be successful enough to be listened to. I think about these things regularly because I live them – every day. I am acutely aware of how society treats people like me, regardless of what I have or haven't done.

After a few jobs, I joined Deloitte. Being the world's largest professional services firm, I was excited to do something different in an organization of this scale. I paved out history-making roles at Deloitte that had never existed before and along with the mentorship of one of the most amazing women I've ever met, Jackie Henry (I hope you're reading, Jackie!), I made true meaningful change happen at Deloitte. I spent time across almost all of their member firms in North and South Europe, training senior leaders on privilege, igniting tailored diversity and inclusion (D&I) strategies in these regions and creating networks of senior leaders backing inclusion. During this time, I really found my feet. Working at Deloitte was a transformative experience for me because I was influencing some of the most senior stakeholders in the organization. This allowed me to grow into being comfortable with holding my own, whilst challenging and educating those around me. This was a journey for me. The Sheree of 2020/21 is not the same person as she was in 2016. I have faced a lot of friction in my career – both because of what I'm aiming to do and also because I am a young woman of colour who does not look or sound like the people who are deemed worthy of listening to. I've been told on many occasions to wait my turn or to not try because someone else (who was viewed as better) tried and it didn't work. I never took that advice.

Influencing senior partners and senior leadership at a professional services firm was not always easy or something I was always comfortable with. Hierarchy is embedded into every fibre of a Big 4's being for the most part. Where I found my strengths was that I had a lot of senior leadership experience through my Women Who Code work. I walked the strange line of being senior outside of Deloitte but not senior within Deloitte. Whilst that was complicated, it meant I had the skills to influence senior management (which is an anomaly in your early 20s). I'll be honest and say I was never scared or terrified of talking to these people though. I spent a lot of time being aware of what I brought to the table and how I would better this person's experience too, as well as them bettering mine. I also live by the motto that everyone is just a person, they are just likely paid more than me. But at the end of the day, they are just a person – the same as me.

I did have some great allies in Deloitte who were aware of the privilege they had as senior leaders and actively advocated for me to be in rooms that I wouldn't have been in, saying my name when I wasn't around and purposefully giving me opportunities that allowed me to grow.

From Deloitte, I've moved on to other organizations that have allowed me to really put this confidence to use – educating, building things from the ground up and defining new equitable environments from scratch.

This is why this book is important – it is possible to effect change and make your own work more inclusive. My life's work is teaching people (at various levels of seniority within companies) so that they can effect change too, because they are empowered to do so.

I am 29 now, and in the last seven years I have won lots of different awards for my services to the industry and the impact of this is not lost on me. When I started out on this journey, I never could have contemplated I would be where I am now. But I am excited to use this confidence in reaching entirely new goals that I haven't even thought of yet. There are days where my background and experiences shape me for the worse, but there are days when

I am so empowered by how I've been able to push through and make true impacts for people around me (and myself).

I am underrepresented, yet privileged. I am of Sri Lankan origin, but I was adopted at three weeks old by an Irish couple. I have been raised in rural Northern Ireland, where currently 2 per cent of the population are from the BAME (Black, Asian and Minority Ethnic) community. With the exception of my brother, I did not have connections to any people of colour. Throughout my life, I have faced racism and bias due to my skin colour, sexism due to my gender and in my professional career, age bias due to holding a leadership role at a relatively young age.

I had a complicated childhood tainted with bullying, mental emotional abuse and narcissism in the people around me, which has led to mental health issues. However, I had food and shelter, went to school, obtained financial grants and attended the university of my choice, achieved a degree and gained a career I am passionate about, which sees me now financially stable. I am a cisgender, straight woman, who can comfortably talk about their partner with ease. I do not have any visible disabilities. From my name and accent, you cannot tell I am a person of colour until you see me or my photo. Due to my experience and accolades, I have earned the privilege of being heard and, more importantly, listened to.

Being adopted has made all of the above feasible and within the realms of the possible. Without that one part of my journey, my life would have been very different. I have been on a journey back to Sri Lanka and found my biological mother and it is clear our lives are stark contrasts.

My career is now dedicated to ensuring people are aware of the fantastic opportunities available to them, making certain that all humans are able to benefit from these and reach their full career potential.

In this book, I want to share the different insights I have, why it's important to think about inclusion day-to-day and not just in our work environments. Embracing diverse opinions and voices is something we need to do in all aspects of our lives. Fostering inclusive environments does not just mean in work, but translates also to our homes and how we move around in our daily lives.

In this book we will talk about how bias has shaped society and the systemic reasons that have caused these inequalities, how we can have these conversations with merit both in work and in our daily lives, and put into practice actionable changes that make for a fairer and more equitable society.

We can all spend a little time understanding how our backgrounds have shaped us and why they have brought us to where we are. Thinking about the things you might have or not have – but importantly, considering other people's backgrounds too.

Who are you and how did you get to where you are today? Has the way society treats you changed you? Was it for the better or worse? What about at work? Do you see or feel people being treated differently based on different characteristics or needs? Do you see your processes working better for some rather than working fairly for all? Do you see a lot of people like you in work or do you see the opposite? These questions must be considered in your business and your work. Have a think.

References

Aizenman, N (2020) [accessed 13 December 2020] US Missionary With No Medical Training Settles Suit over Child Deaths at Her Center, NPR, 31 July [Online] www.npr.org/sections/goatsandsoda/2020/07/31/897773 274/u-s-missionary-with-no-medical-training-settles-suit-over-child-deaths-at-her-ce?t=1604397437929 (archived at https://perma.cc/ A7QZ-FZ6G)

Levy, A (2020) [accessed 13 December 2020] Missionary on Trial, *The New Yorker*, 7 April [Online] www.newyorker.com/magazine/ 2020/04/13/a-missionary-on-trial (archived at https://perma.cc/2CLS-UDY6)

Mwesigwa, A and Beaumont, P (2019) [accessed 13 December 2020] Did Children Die Because of 'White Saviour' Renee Bach? *The Guardian*, 17 October [Online] www.theguardian.com/global-development/2019/oct/17/did-a-white-saviours-evangelical-zeal-turn-deadly-uganda-renee-bach-serving-his-children (archived at https://perma.cc/85Z3-5RPK)

Wikipedia (2020) [accessed 13 December 2020] Demography of Northern Ireland [Online] https://en.wikipedia.org/wiki/Demography_of_Northern_Ireland#Ethnicity (archived at https://perma.cc/YF4T-XA8T)

CHAPTER TWO

Why diversity and inclusion aren't there yet

This chapter will focus on:

- What is diversity?
- What is inclusion?
- What is diversity and inclusion, together?
- Where are we in society?
- What effect does this have on business and why hasn't this been prioritized?

What is diversity?

Diversity has a lot of different meanings to different people. To me, it means that there is an array of differences existing in one place, together. That the current state of what is happening is diverse.

The state of being diverse is quite a statement. What does that mean? How does a group or organization achieve that state (remember that people are not singularly diverse, groups are). Diversity has become so much of a buzzword that, at times, it loses meaning for people. When we hear something so regularly, if we don't fully engage or listen to the meaning behind the phrasing, it's very easy to just discount it. But this is something that is so important to engage with.

Diversity in groups allows the blend of perspectives, experiences and ideas, on the same topic or conversation. When we live, socialize or work with people from all different backgrounds, we ultimately hear perspectives that we may never have heard before. It is important to remember that different characteristics like gender, ethnicity, whether we have visible or invisible disabilities, are a member of the LGBT+ community and more play a huge role in our perspectives, experiences and ideas. Society treats people differently based on many of these characteristics, both singularly and combined. I'll give you an example. Think about this scenario in your head.

You are going down the street after a night out, you're by yourself and you're cold. You have a hoodie in your bag, so you put it on. Who wouldn't? What thoughts are going through your head as you move down the street? If you are a white man, perhaps you are just thinking about getting home. It is cold after all! If you are a Black man, maybe you're thinking about getting home and also worrying about the connotations and stereotypes that people make about Black men in hoodies. You just want to get home, but you know people judge you differently because of your skin colour and something as small as a sweater that keeps your ears warm.

Organizations like 56 Black Men and Humanize My Hoodie have dedicated their work to challenging the stereotypes that Black and brown men face in society. If you are a man who is a member of the LGBT+ community, maybe you're rushing to get home and also worrying that someone might stop you who is homophobic and might start a fight with you.

If you are a woman, maybe you are just trying to get home but you are also worrying about being a woman out late at night. So maybe you have decided to share your location with someone you trust, or call someone so you don't feel fully alone.

I appreciate that this is a serious example, but it is important. And of course, you may not relate to any of these scenarios, but it is worth trying to put yourself in that mindset for others. Let's look at this from another lens too.

You are excited about a potential new job. You have got all the skills and this would be a great role for you – and there is a nice pay increase too! You get the call about the next stage – it is a video interview. What is your first thought? Take a second to think. Is it 'fantastic, this gives me a chance to shine?' Maybe you are a little nervous, but still excited? Or is it a realization that you don't have any equipment to take a video call? Maybe you don't own earphones or a laptop, or don't even have a safe, quiet space to be able to take the call?

In a study of 71,000 students, researchers concluded that students from wealthier backgrounds are on the whole more comfortable with all stages of the hiring process. Students from poorer backgrounds are more likely to drop out after live video interviews (Doherty, 2019). Here's an example from a work-place perspective.

You are going for a promotion and you feel like you've done well this year. Last year, your feedback was that you needed to be more confident and assertive in your deliverables. You've purposefully taken more ownership and led with direction to showcase that you are more than capable of this. Your promotion review comes up. What is the feedback you receive this year? If you're a man, perhaps it is that you've done well, you've shown leadership and it's clear that you have done well and can continue to do well. Your team has met their goals and appreciated your direction. You feel confident you're going for promotion.

If you're a woman, perhaps it is that you have been too bossy and that you've not shown your leadership skills for long enough. That you've not been a team player and have been too assertive. After all, we don't promote potential, just proof.

There are barriers that some of us never have or will experience. But many folks do experience these and it gives them an entirely different perspective on life. It is important to note that a person is not 'diverse'. Diversity is having a group of people from different backgrounds. It is not calling a Black woman 'diverse' because she is not a white man. Remember that means we are putting the focus on white and male being the 'norm' or the 'standard' we should work to. Groups of people can be diverse; a person however is not diverse on their own.

We have spoken about what diversity is, but what is inclusion?

Inclusion can be defined as being included – being embedded in and actively involved in what is going on.

'Being included' feels pretty self-explanatory. We can probably all remember times when we have felt included and when we haven't. Think about some of them now. What are the things that make a difference in you feeling included and you feeling excluded?

Feeling included can mean many different things to different people. But, ultimately, it is usually something that shows a sign of respect at the core of whatever the action is. Respect and being respectful to one another play a huge role in inclusion. Do you feel more included when someone respects your input, your voice, your ideas, your views on the world? Hopefully the answer is yes. Think about what times are the most enjoyable when you are with your friends, with work colleagues, when you're at school or with your family? When you feel like you are listened to, can contribute to conversations and actively bounce off each other.

That isn't to say that inclusion means we can't disagree – we absolutely can and we should when we don't align. However, again, this can be done respectfully.

What is diversity and inclusion, together?

When we think about inclusion, regularly we think of community and networking. Feeling included is feeling like you 'belong' somewhere because you have found something in common with the people around you – that can be in work and also in your personal life.

For me, finding a sense of inclusion and belonging means people respecting my opinions and valuing the input I bring. But it is also much more than doing that just on the surface level. There is a difference in speaking and being heard. I would like you to think about that difference.

Speaking into a vacuum means no one is listening, but you are still going to the emotional effort of sharing. However, is there any point other than it potentially being a little cathartic? Some of us only speak when it is relevant to do so, so by that logic we would like folks to listen. Speaking and being heard is exactly that. People are listening, giving back their thoughts and engaging with you. As a senior leader in industry, this is super important to me.

Inclusion from a community sense is only one side of the coin, though. Inclusion in processes and procedures is just as important – if not, this is the equivalent of speaking and not being heard. Personally, I have felt this on numerous occasions. Being brought into the room to deliver and share but not having people put into practice what they've heard. Or being hired into a senior role only for the organization to change its mind and descope the role less than one year later. Or rolling out a strategy and having senior leaders parrot the work I have just said instead of giving appropriate credit and amplification. A community can want to be inclusive, but if procedures or leadership behaviours fall short, then we are not doing what we need to do.

How easily we can exist successfully in organizations is a good measure of inclusion. Can people of all backgrounds reach the opportunities where you work? Do people from all backgrounds get promoted or do those in similar groups move ahead more than others? What does your leadership team look like?

A good piece of analysis to do is on the tenured (those who have been at your organization for a long period of time and/or those who have progressed from junior to mid-tier/senior in this one company) vs experienced-hire employee (those whom you hire in a mid-tier/senior level because of prior experience elsewhere) experience. Your organization will likely have both and it's highly probable your experienced-hire pool is more diverse than your tenured. One reason you hire experienced people is because you have a gap to fill. The knowledge doesn't exist internally and it is needed to continue to succeed or progress. Bringing in people from different backgrounds and experiences is great – it's what we need and it stops an echo chamber forming. What isn't good is hiring for 'culture fit'. 'Culture fit' is hiring people based on how well you think they will match with everyone else – will they just click into place, think in a similar way and therefore cause less friction?

'Culture fit' is toxic. It means you bring in those people and expect them to fit your way only. What you get when you hire someone externally is different ideas and experience from an array of environments, which is why you will have hired them. Joining any new organization is stressful and people should be given time to settle into a way that works for both them and the company. However, this works both ways.

You cannot hire experienced employees and expect them to not bring that experience and knowledge of what does and doesn't work for them and the environments around them. There is a balance to be had there – employees must be willing to learn new ways of working but so should the company. If you hire people in and force them into fitting a mould that is so very clearly not going to fit, they'll leave and you're back at square one.

If your company has 1) a high turnover of staff and 2) a short average tenure of experienced hires, consider why. Are they being welcomed, respected and listened to? Or have you brought them in and disregarded them because they are 'different'. Let's not forget the lens of gender, ethnicity, etc – they matter, a lot.

Create a leaver's survey (with option for one-to-one leaver's interview) that asks why people are leaving, if anything could have been done to make them want to stay, ask them to rate middle management and senior leadership separately and if there are any suggestions they'd want to see changed. Once you have this, using your employee's 'date joined company' data, put a lens on this for tenure vs experienced hires (and an additional lens for gender and ethnicity), analyse it every quarter, giving you meaningful trends to have conversations. If you're not analysing this data to this level, you're not utilizing it meaningfully.

Once you have this analysis, there must be accountability. If there is a trend of senior experienced folks leaving, what will you do? You should discuss this making it clear what you've found out and what the main reasons are for leaving. There is potentially a culture problem. If you now realize there is a culture problem of your company not being as inclusive for some as others, what will you do?

You can either do nothing (don't do that!) or you can start talking about this transparently. There will need to be discussions with tenured staff to understand their views, experiences and ideas too. There must be safe space discussions to share perceptions – consider using an anonymous polling tool like Mentimeter that allows for live interaction whilst keeping psychological safety. Afterwards, there must be a clear understanding of how onboarding works, how communication styles work for everyone and what happens when they don't (a code of conduct is a great way to do this; we'll talk about that in a bit...).

There will be times when people revert back – it's human nature. You must be ready to have the difficult conversations when that happens. As a manager or leader, if you cannot deliver difficult news, then you aren't suitable for your job. Everything isn't always positive and poor behaviour will need to be called out professionally.

Experienced and tenured should work hand in hand because you need both. For this to work in sync, there must be clear accountability, communication and support for all. If the reason for someone not being good enough is 'They don't think like us' or 'They don't do things our way', remember: that's why you hired them. Internally, you don't have the knowledge they have, so you need it. Yes, balance is needed on working styles for everyone involved, but be honest. If you hear this and your trends in the leaver's analysis backs it up, you'll see gatekeeping of who is/isn't good enough. Usually with tenured employees, there will be group think, as quite often companies do not have a diverse employee base to begin with. Therefore, the tenured group may be more homogeneous.

This means the knock-on effect is that you have hired a more diverse group of people for the experience you need; they're not the same as the folks who are already there; you don't like that; they feel disrespected/unwelcome; they leave; you're back at square one.

You need both. Remember that. Use your data to spot trends, be accountable and fuel your diversity, equity and inclusion strategy.

Where are we in society?

To truly make solutions or organizations work inclusively, their processes and creations must be challenged from perspectives outside of the majority demographics they serve. Otherwise, we create an echo-chamber version of inclusion where a solution may only work for men and not women, white people and not people of colour, non-disabled people and not disabled people, etc. When we have real, genuine inclusion, we have been able to challenge all barriers, discrimination and potential intolerance.

That is no easy task but it is absolutely one we should take on. There are many business benefits to embracing diversity and fostering environments of inclusion, as we will see in Chapter 7 on Demanding more from our leaders. Companies in the top quartile for gender diversity outperform their competitors by 15% and those in the top quartile for ethnic diversity outperform their competitors by 35% (Hunt, Layton and Prince, 2015). What this means is when we bring different voices and experiences into the one room, we have different lenses and viewpoints on the one problem or issue. By hearing these different experiences and viewpoints, we are able to create solutions that meet the needs of a diverse society. Without this, we are making assumptions on what this group needs – and assumption and fact are two very different things.

What is the effect inclusion has on businesses and why hasn't this been prioritized?

When diversity and inclusion work together, we have environments and societies where everyone is included and supported, regardless of what their background is. One without the other creates a disengaged population.

Think about how it feels if you speak, you share your emotions, you vote for something that matters to you and nothing changes or no one responds. Diversity and inclusion together mean we actively do the work to reach out and embrace those from all different backgrounds, listening to them to understand what inclusion means to them and then putting it into action. Here are some examples.

Religion

Where you work, everyone typically has a meeting on a Friday at midday where people catch up, hear what everyone is up to and help create friendships throughout the organization. It's a great way for everyone to wind down and finish the week on a positive. No one ever really misses out on this, unless they're really busy or want to give it a miss.

You've just hired a new workmate and they are Muslim. They are great and it has been lovely to have some new perspectives on the team. But it comes to Friday each week and you notice they are never at the wrap-up meeting. You have never thought why or considered maybe there's a reason why they are continually missing.

As you may know, some folks who are Muslim pray just after noon on a Friday and this prayer can be an integral part of their faith. If the meeting was made earlier or just slightly later, they could also join in on the meeting and catch up with everyone. If we consider this small change, we make a big impact.

This is just one small example. We must do serious thinking and analysis when it comes to all of the processes and procedures we use. How do they positively or negatively affect certain groups? What does the data tell you? What will you do with the information you decipher? Inclusion is about structure and making no assumptions about the successes and failures we and our work may have.

What is important to consider now is the impact on a society that has so regularly not prioritized inclusion or the effects on underrepresented groups. Where are we right now?

When you think about society where you are from right now, what are the main words you think of? The statistics and perspectives I will share are largely based on the UK and the United States, but I want you to think about your own perspective too.

Gender

The first lens we will talk about is how a lack of gender inclusion has allowed a bias-shaped society to prosper and a society that is not built for women to succeed. Let's start from the top.

In 2019, the number of men called Michael outnumbered the number of women chairing FTSE firms (Turvill, 2019). That means that in the majority of the world's most influential and ground-breaking organizations, women are not present as chairs, where senior leadership and responsibility lies. In 2019, just five companies had women chairs, despite many being vocal supporters of prioritizing gender inclusion.

Having a voice at decision-making tables allows you to shift, change and voice opinions that otherwise may not be present. When we actively bring differing opinions and perspectives into the one room, we're able to put varying lenses on the same problem or solution, therefore allowing us to come to conclusions that more closely represent the people we're aiming to serve.

We see a huge disparity in the number of women reaching senior leadership positions and regularly the reasons are around caring responsibilities; however, there are many systematic barriers that cause real issues in stopping progress in this way. More than half of women in tech leave the industry by the mid-point of their career, which is more than double the rate of men (Bayern, 2019). A Capital One study (Welson-Rossman, 2020) shows that the main reasons women currently leave tech include weak management support (23 per cent), lack of opportunity (20 per cent) and lack of work–life balance (22 per cent).

The mid-point of a career is typically in management, and right before joining senior leadership, moving closer to the executive layer at the top of an organization. Typically at this age, some women are having children or starting to have families. When having biological children, there is a given that the person carrying a child will need and want to take time away from work to heal both physically and mentally. Supporting partners may also want to take time to bond and support; however, it is important to remember the very real stress a pregnancy puts on the human body.

When we need to take time away from work, work doesn't stop. Things continue to change and evolve with decisions being made. Having time away ultimately means people are out of the loop through no fault of their own. When we haven't prioritized inclusion, these people get lost in the cracks in the system, and we haven't primed managers well enough to support folks transitioning back into the workplace whilst balancing brand new priorities. Consider even how hard it can be to get back into the swing of things after a long holiday? Now consider this when there are new things to balance, new health issues to prioritize and more.

Work–life balance affects everyone of all genders. When we force people to view work as their main priority, we are driving them to make decisions that put work first and not their health or families. Work–life balance is especially important when we consider the dynamics of men and those who do not identify as men, understanding how society views women as caretakers and therefore expected to take on more caring responsibilities. This societal inequality maps to our day-to-day and how we work.

A very real example of this inequality materialized during the Covid-19 pandemic in the spring of 2020, where a study surfaced that women make up the majority of workers in the health and social care sector – 70 per cent in 104 countries analysed by the World Health Organization (World Economic Forum, 2020). Women also work two-thirds of minimum wage jobs, putting them at increased risk of unemployment (in the case of all-but-closed retail and hospitality industries) and illness (in the case of essential jobs like grocery cashiers). These statistics cannot be ignored because they shape how we live day-to-day and how we work.

In the tech space, many voice-recognition technologies at first did not recognize female voices (despite many AI assistant's voices being female) because the design teams did not include women (McMillan, 2011). Many voice-recognition technologies today do not recognize different accents because they were designed by native English speakers and were not made by a team with different backgrounds. If we build diverse representation into the teams making our ground-breaking technologies, then we are more likely to have a successful business.

Ethnicity

When we put the lens of ethnicity onto this problem, we can see a similar story. People of colour are not prioritized in society, and therefore their needs from systems are not included or prioritized in the same way their white counterparts' needs are.

In 2019, '77% of White people were employed, compared with 65% of people from all other ethnic groups combined. The difference in employment rates between the White ethnic group and all other ethnic groups combined went down from 16% in 2004 to 12% in 2018' (Gov England, Wales and Scotland, 2019). These statistics are important because they highlight a bias in many different areas of society. We have to be honest with how society has allowed race to benefit some and actively detract from others.

White people make up the majority groups both in leadership and in the workforce in general. Sixty-eight per cent of white British households own their own homes, compared with 74 per cent of Indian households. However, households in the Black African (20 per cent) and Arab (17 per cent) ethnic groups had the lowest rates of home ownership. In every socioeconomic group and age group, white British households were more likely to own their own homes than all ethnic minority households combined in every region in England.

Think about the barriers to owning your own home. You ordinarily need to 1) have a stable income, 2) be applicable for a mortgage and 3) be able to meet a threshold of income to sustain a household. We can see that the employment rate of all non-white ethnic groups has decreased, so can we expect a similar trend when it comes to homeowning too?

If we think about structural barriers for people of colour, we have to accept that racism exists and we can only be anti-racist if we actively challenge whiteness as the norm. Out of all ethnic groups, Black people face a unique type of racism from both white and other non-Black ethnicities. Black people have been enslaved and abused throughout history. There must be an acceptance from non-Black people about the very real effects this has had on society, job opportunities, life opportunities, a view of self-worth and more. White supremacy is a very real thing and its effects are deadly.

It's important we look at the consequences of groups of people being actively excluded from working in industries such as technology. Technology is used by all of us, whether it be registering to vote, getting on the train using contactless payment, ordering your shopping online and more. When something is used by society as an ingrained part of our lives, it must be considered from these various different lenses. In 2019, a facial detection system used by the UK Government rejected a passport photograph of a young Black man because it mistook his lips for an open mouth. Passport photographs require the subject to have a plain expression with their mouth closed (Cook, 2019). The issue here is that the data set used to test the system didn't have enough diversity in it, therefore this Black man's mouth wasn't registered correctly. There wasn't a diverse team behind the creation of a product that needs to serve millions of people, therefore it has gaps.

If we don't challenge the bias that exists in society, it directly seeps into our work and programmes. Simply saying 'we're not racist' isn't good enough. Another example of this is the use of ImageNet, a trove of 14 million images hand-labelled by humans as a training guide for AIs, that recently classified Black faces as 'blackamoor', 'negroid' or 'black person', while results from Caucasian faces varied more widely as 'researcher', 'scientist' or 'singer' (Bernal and Dodds, 2019).

There are many technology solutions that have had negative effects or simply do not work for women and people of colour (don't forget that cross-section of women of colour!). Both of these groups are severely underrepresented in industry. Remember that technology is a heavily white man-dominated space and, therefore, the teams developing and testing the solution are not always diverse.

Many of us use voice recognition – maybe it's your Amazon Alexa, or Siri on your phone, or for voice-assisted technology for those who need it.

Facial recognition software is becoming more and more commonplace; however, it consistently has issues when recognizing people of colour. In a recent study (Buolamwini *et al*, 2018) of using recognition software to identify gender, the error rate is significantly higher if the subject is a person of colour. When the person in the photo is a white man, the software is right 99 per cent of the time. But the darker the skin, the more errors arise – up to nearly 35 per cent for images of darker-skinned women.

Society directly affects how we view people – whether they are 'good or bad', 'acceptable or unacceptable', 'worthy of hate or not'. During the Covid-19 pandemic, the rise of anti-Asian hate crimes became very apparent, with people of Asian descent being attacked physically and verbally in the street (Anti-Defamation League, 2020). Let's remember that these stereotypes and issues will manifest in where and how we work, if we do not actively challenge them. Being idle is not enough to push through the effects.

Disability

According to the World Health Organization:

1.3 billion people are affected by some form of blindness and visual impairment. This represents 17% of the world's population. 466 million people have a disabling deafness and hearing loss. This represents 6% of the world's population. About 200 million people have an intellectual disability (IQ below 75). This represents 2.6% of the world's population. 75 million people need a wheelchair on a daily basis. This represents 1% of the world's population. (Wagner, 2019)

The world has not been created with disabled needs in mind and this has serious consequences. In the summer of 2020, Twitter rolled out voice-notes to an array of users – a nifty way to record a message for your followers. However, it was rolled out with no option for closed captioning, meaning that those with hearing disabilities or impairments couldn't use or utilize the feature. This was raised swiftly as a breach of the Americans With Disabilities Act, which was signed into law 30 years ago, when Twitter responded that this was an 'early version of the feature'. The key point here is that accessibility is not an add on – it is a necessity from the beginning.

Think about how you get in and out of work if you are able-bodied. Do you drive a car, get a bus or if you're in a city, get an underground tube? In London, Transport for London claims that 79 out of 270 Tube stations have step-free access (Transport for London, 2020). In Zone 1 there are only nine stations with step-free access from street to platform, and of these only four stations are step-free from the street to all trains running through those stations. Think about what this means for wheelchair users, especially those travelling in Zone 1. Also consider the regularity of tube-station lifts being out of order.

It's important to also consider the extra financial cost of being disabled. Scope completed a study across 21,000 people (with 4,000 disabled people represented) showing that, on average, disabled people have an extra monthly cost of £583 and that a disabled person's extra costs are equivalent to almost half of their income (not including housing costs) (Scope, 2019). An additional cost to something that is out of your control.

From the Inclusive Boards' (2019) Disability in Senior Leadership Toolkit, we can see that, of:

> C-suite members, EY and the Valuable 500 found that only 7% of executives reported having an impairment while 56% said the topic of disability rarely or never comes up on their leadership agenda. Given that 18.6% of the working age population is disabled, there is a sizable disparity between the proportion of disabled people able to work and those reaching senior leadership.

They also surveyed the boards of every funded sports organization in the UK and found that only 5 per cent of board members consider themselves to be disabled, compared to around 22 per cent in the wider UK population (Inclusive Boards, 2019). There is a barrier to entry for those who have readily been forgotten or viewed as 'lesser' by society.

Sexual orientation

Studies have indicated that 35 per cent of LGBT+ employees throughout organizations in the UK hide that they are LGBT+ in the workplace for fear of discrimination (Stonewall, 2018). Think about what this means for a person and their mental health. Do you worry about how you'll be viewed or treated in work based on who your partner is or what your interests are? Do you feel comfortable sharing your weekend plans with people in work because you don't mind talking about your girlfriend, boyfriend, wife or husband? Think about the extra emotional labour of having to come out every time you move companies, you get a new manager or you start to work on a new project? This is a decision that LGBT+ folks have to consider.

In the United States only one in five US companies offer paid family leave for LGBT+ employees (LGBT Map, 2018), when this is commonplace for heterosexuals. In Northern Ireland, gay marriage was only passed as legal at the start of 2020, with political parties opposing it for decades, with religion being used as their main reason to oppose it. These decisions make a clear point – LGBT+ families and partnerships are lesser than those of their heterosexual counterparts.

The acronym 'LGBT+' covers a wide range of people and experiences. I want us to dip into the 'T' here for a moment (and we'll delve into this deeper later, too). Transgender people are discriminated at much higher rates than other members of the LGBT+ community, and very specifically Black trans women. According to the Human Rights Campaign, as of June 2020, there were 14 transgender or gender non-conforming people fatally shot or killed by other types of violence that were not related to shootings. In 2019, the number was 26, the majority of whom were Black trans women (Kelly, 2020). There is an important note here that trans women face a unique blend of sexism and homophobia, and those who are Black face racism added into this. Black women in general are one of the most ill-treated groups in society and being a Black trans women creates another element of vulnerability and reason for attack.

Whilst policy makers and activists have made progress for equal marriage and other LGBT+-focused rights, trans rights have very much remained stagnant and still. A common phrase of 'no one is free until we are all free' is poignant here. We will talk about this in more detail in Chapter 4 on intersectionality.

Socioeconomic background

Socioeconomic status is an economic and sociological combined total of your work experience and of your or your family's economic and social position in relation to others in society. Socioeconomic status plays a crucial role in diversity and inclusion – being from poorer backgrounds changes the opportunities afforded to you by society. It is entirely fair to see that it is harder to succeed in business being from a background where this isn't the norm.

Personally, I identify with this a lot. I've shared my story at the start of this book and I am acutely aware of how this has played a role in where I am now. I have had to push myself hard, taking lots of grants and bursaries to go to university (only to still be in debt) and go on the learning curve of what it means to be in an industry that none of my family was in. We must consider how we actively include those from poorer backgrounds and there have been many examples where this has not happened.

In 2020, in the midst of the Covid-19 pandemic, A Level exams were cancelled. These are the exams in the UK that define which university you are able to attend and if you're accepted based on your predicted grades. Due to students being unable to sit these exams because schools were closed for safety reasons, the UK government overseeing Scotland, Wales, England and Northern Ireland rolled out a new system to predict students' grades based on schools' previous exam averages and scores. When A Level grades were announced in England, Wales and Northern Ireland, nearly 40 per cent were lower than teachers' assessments, with similar issues in Scotland. In England, specifically, 3 per cent of students were marked down by two grades (BBC, 2020). That means the system actively changed people's grades to the extent that they were no longer able to attend their university of choice because an algorithm decided that they could only possibly score what students in previous years had done. From a social mobility aspect, it is notable that the downgrading affected state schools much more than the private sector. This means that high-achieving students from poorer backgrounds were penalized, with some having predicted grades such as 'AAB' changed to 'EED'. Protests ensued and after a week of turmoil, the government reversed their decision. This is all well and good, but by this stage many universities had already allocated places, meaning some students lost out on their dream university choices.

This is what happens when people in power and authority do not care or consider the most vulnerable in our society.

Having few or no diverse senior leadership teams has very real consequences. We have the knock-on effect of processes that have been developed that do not work for underrepresented groups. You will regularly hear about being 'the only', but it has a real emotional tax to be that person.

Being 'the only' means you are the only person like you in the room. Maybe you are the only woman, the only person with a disability, the only person of colour and so on – or a combination of a number of things. Success for people like this can be an indicator of a system that has prioritized inclusion; however, if they are in the minority, it's important to remember that the success of one does not mean the opportunity of success for all.

If we know all of these things, why are they still a problem? Why do we have such a similar makeup of people across leadership teams, almost irrespective of industries? The short answer is that there is not enough leadership buy-in to change it. There aren't enough people backing systematic change – the change that really does mean we accept what we've done isn't good enough and that we need to dismantle it and start again. It's difficult knowing that we may have benefited from something that actively has disadvantaged others like the colour of your skin. If you are white, your skin tone is a benefit to you. If you are a person of colour, it is the opposite.

Structural change involves spending a lot of time looking at ourselves and our own privileges (we'll talk more about that later!) and shortcomings. It is not easy, but it's important to understand how life is experienced differently by different people. It is important when we do that, we remember that gender, sexual orientation, ethnicity, disability, neurodiversity and more play a huge role in those experiences.

When we talk about inclusion, we must talk about inclusion of those that we do not directly or indirectly identify with. If we only care about inclusion for those similar to us, then we don't care at all. We cannot make changes that simply create a new type of exclusion.

People are drawn to those similar to themselves. Think about who you surround yourself with – your partner, your friends, the people you enjoy being around. Is there any commonality you have with them? This may be fine in our daily lives, but how does it affect businesses? We'll delve into these different types of biases a little later.

So far, diversity and inclusion efforts have been heavily focused on gender diversity. Now, women come from all different backgrounds, but these efforts have more positively affected white women than women of any other group. Between 2016 and 2018, there were a total of 230 new board seats within Fortune 500 firms. Across these roles, white women obtained 124, Black women 32, Asian women 17 and Hispanic women only 4 seats (Catalyst, 2018). When we aren't clear about what diversity and inclusion is, how we're going to tackle it and why, we end up with biased outcomes. Good intentions are not good enough. We have to understand how prioritizing only groups that we or senior leadership directly identify with creates an environment of exclusion. Privileged inclusion is when we focus only on the underrepresented groups of people that we directly or indirectly identify with, where we deem them important enough to care about. This usually means that white, non-disabled, economically privileged, cisgendered, straight women are the only people that are being focused on in our diversity and inclusion work.

I'd like you to spend a few minutes thinking about what embracing diversity and fostering inclusion mean to you. Write it down – what are the things that make you feel included, both in your day-to-day and in work? Rate out of 10 how included you feel in society and in your work life.

Now think about if they are the same for someone else? Are they very different for people of a different gender and different ethnicity to you? Do you think that person would rate their score the same? Run this exercise in your teams at work.

I sat down with Vanessa Vallely OBE, CEO and Founder of WeAreTheCity to discuss diversity, inclusion and how both must work in tandem for real impact. Vanessa's corporate experience stems from a 25-year career in banking, holding roles such as Head of Governance, Business Management & Chief Operating Officer. WeAreTheCity was launched in April 2008 and has 120,000 professional women members in the UK, with a 40,000 base in India. They work with over 150 corporate clients enabling them to attract, retain and develop their female talent. Given Vanessa's extensive professional services career, I asked her about her reasons for pivoting into launching organizations dedicated to helping people like her. Was there a turn point moment? She said:

It was a kind of utopian moment actually. I started working in the city at 16 and was very, very driven. More for the fact that I was told all the things I couldn't do. I've had a bit in between my teeth to prove people wrong and it served me well. I was very career orientated for the best part of 20 years and I always had a trait that I'd like to help others, but it didn't really come to me from a leadership perspective until I got into more senior roles.

I had a moment I was sitting in a leadership meeting with investment managers and it was a room full of men competing with each other. And I just looked at the women that were on my team at the time and thought, 'how do I get them into this room?' because I felt like I got there by accident. Some groups already existed; however, they were primarily for women who were from higher economic backgrounds, whose husbands all knew each other and needed referrals to join – they were all lovely – but I didn't see myself in them as a woman who grew up in a lower economic background. The final push was my husband buying me the website and domain... then we got to work!

Given WeAreTheCity serves 120,000 women in the UK and 40,000 in India, and the fact that women are not a monolith, I asked Vanessa how she ensured they were able to serve women of all backgrounds (more on intersectionality later!) and provide them with the support they needed. She said:

Our membership is very wide and spread across different diverse backgrounds. That is because of four key considerations.

Firstly, when I opened our doors, we set no criteria. So there was no way anyone could deselect themselves. And you know, as women, we're quite good at that. This was open for everyone.

Secondly, consider your wording and descriptions – we're open to all women and ensure that our branding and wording reflects this. There are no barriers. For example, for our awards, we took out age limits so everyone can be included. In our marketing, we have always been acutely aware of ensuring all women can see themselves on our website and social media or in the array of previous winners in our awards. We ensure we lend our platform to people and businesses of all sizes – not just those who are well established.

Thirdly, always remember you do not know everything. No one does. We are reached out to regularly and if there is something that we think we're not best placed to help with, we will recommend someone who is. This is bigger than just you. Likewise if we are running an event to support a specific community, we will consult with that community first to make sure we're doing it right.

Fourthly, consider who you work with and why. We didn't search for sponsors for the first seven years – anything we wanted to do, I paid for. Now, we're in a position to choose who we work with and only work with organizations that really care about supporting women in industry.

Through these different initiatives WeAreTheCity has impact for women of all backgrounds. Vanessa's work and her organization are actively sought out by different companies to help bolster their diversity, equity and inclusion (DEI) efforts in the gender-focused spaces. Given so many organizations are at varying different stages on their diversity and inclusion journey, I asked Vanessa how she manages these differences in journeys and progress. She said:

Companies are on a journey and we know that. Typically, we expect organizations to work with us once they have a decent DEI strategy in place, where we are there to help support and empower the women in their businesses. There have been companies who weren't at the right stage for us so we have recommended them to take some action, and work with DEI consultants first... then they come back to us when they're in a better position to make a real impact with our community.

And lastly, you must take the ability to educate yourself rather than the laziness of asking someone within that community those questions. We're learning all the time. I feel very passionate about this and am frustrated when I hear people saying that they cannot find talented women or people from other underrepresented groups. It's not difficult. We do it every single year.

I've known Vanessa for years and we've discussed before the barriers we've both faced in our careers and how they have affected us. This is what she said when I asked her about the biases she has herself faced in her journey:

> I've faced bias (certainly earlier in my career) around my accent and my postcode. I struggled to find jobs when I was younger because I was from Hackney. People judged me because of that and put blockers in front of me because of that. Some managers would correct my vocabulary and no matter what role I was in, even the senior ones, there would still be comments or something to remind you where you came from. It can knock your confidence because there were always a multitude of questions around where I lived, where I went to university (I didn't) and so on. I used to go to elocution lessons to change my accent. But now, I don't care. The older I get, the better I have been able to handle these people. I have rebuttals and I am determined to continue to pave a way for women of all backgrounds.

Vanessa's passion is palpable – it is clear how important this is to her and why she has dedicated her career to helping women advance. It is notable that Vanessa is a white woman, and I asked her about how she has spent time actively understanding how she can use her own privilege (more on that soon too!) to help those less privileged than her. She said:

> I'm fully accepting that the colour of my skin opens up a lot of doors of opportunity to me. And that is de facto, regardless of the bias people may have towards me because of my gender

or accent. As a white woman, it is really important to know and listen to other people's perspectives and ensure they are showcased on our stages (not just my view). The biggest thing for me is to use your platform to give voice to others. And that goes from me personally too, not just from my business. What I share on my own social media for example, signposting and showcasing people. I actively advocate and sponsor for people too, making sure I am sharing opportunities broadly, actively working to level the playing field.

Lastly, I asked Vanessa what her one piece of advice would be for people trying to demand more from their leaders. She said:

Employee network groups are a great place to start – there can be a fear of calling things out as a single individual and if that is you, there is power in numbers. Raise a collective voice. If you don't have a group, set one up. Also, don't be afraid to go straight to the top – email that Director, VP or CEO. Sometimes organizations are so layered that issues are raised and lost in middle-management. If this happens, go straight to the top.

Vanessa's interview finishes with her saying that:

[t]his isn't about me anymore now. It is now my turn to pass on opportunities and actively advocate for others. There is a new wave of activism from people like you and Seyi (Akiwowo, Founder of Glitch, a non-profit dedicated to eradicating online abuse). It's now my turn to leave my legacy and spend my time pushing and making the way for the next generation. My children are activists and I have raised them to be proactive about discrimination of all types. We cannot rest on the progress we've made now as there is so much more to do. Your generation and the next generation will demand even more action, and that is exactly what we need.

We must demand more from our leaders and from ourselves. Leaders haven't spent enough time thinking about how their decisions affect other people, even just in this small way and then making sure their choices reflect these thoughts. We need more action and less talk.

It's key to remember that inclusion isn't just about being nice or hoping that things fall into place. Exclusion has been deliberately orchestrated, and we must be as deliberate to create inclusion now. Inclusion at work specifically means designing processes and procedures for all, taking meaningful, proactive steps. Some examples of inclusion in practice at work are:

- clear, transparent application questions and processes;
- easy-to-understand promotion criteria;
- two-way communication streams between leadership and all employees;
- open salary frameworks;
- code of conduct;
- psychologically safe grievance process.

Clear, transparent application questions and processes

Your job application questions and processes should be templated and the same for every applicant. Your interviewers should be rating people across the same skills and desired criteria. This is inclusive because it is holding all to the same account and marking – it is clean cut and fair. Creating a framework means we have to mark and ask the same questions of everyone, not choosing different questions based on our own personal bias or interests (which is exclusive). Bias exists in all of us and if we don't create a framework to abide by with ratings, we will double down on what seems good to us.

Your hiring process should be transparent and signposted on your hiring portal so that all applicants know what to expect and when to expect it. If you can't share it on your portal, it should be in the job application or the first email applicants receive confirming their application has been received.

It is all well and good doing this, but you must also invest in training interviewers. Just because someone is at a senior level does not mean they are appropriately skilled or qualified to interview new talent. Being an interviewer means playing a crucial role in shaping the culture of your organization. You are usually one of the first touchpoints an applicant has with your organization and you are supposed to be a role model embodying a positive representation of the organization. Appropriate training across interview techniques, do's and don'ts and inclusive interviewing principles should be developed and made mandatory for all interviewers. If possible, there should be live exercises, with feedback on what interviewers have done well and not so well so people can grow. It's important to note, this may mean that you have to have conversations with those who are simply not suitable to be interviewers. Be prepared for this.

Easy-to-understand promotion criteria

If everyone understands what's clearly expected from them and how to achieve it, we demystify the promotion process. Your promotion criteria should be broken down by level, across skill sets, clearly defining what is expected of each level and why. The language used should be neutral and work should be done to research amongst underrepresented groups if that language genuinely is neutral – no assumptions should be made that it is.

Writing promotion criteria is just one part of the puzzle, though. Words and actions must align. For example, if you put in your promotion criteria that at a senior level you must sponsor those at a more junior level, then you must also have a process in place to gather 360 degree feedback to ensure this is happening.

It is important to recognize that this is a continuous process. When we put in place new processes, we must be open to feedback that they are not quite right. After you roll out a new promotion criteria process, after it goes through its first execution, gather anonymous feedback from employees, with rated responses and open text questions to gather true feedback. Take this feedback away, determine ways to improve, share these openly and put them into practice.

The next step is analysing the impact of the process. You may not have promotion data on gender, ethnicity etc from previous rounds, but that is no excuse to not correct that when moving forward. You cannot truly say if your promotion process is inclusive if you have no data to back up the fact that it does or does not promote a percentage of people from different backgrounds in relation to their representation in the organization.

Two-way communication streams between leadership and all employees

How do you feel when you are caught unaware and unprepared? Do you feel good? Do you feel like you can make the best decisions when you're surprised? More often than not, the answer to that is no.

It may seem strange to say inclusion and corporate communication work hand in hand, but they do. Employees should be kept informed when possible, in a transparent way. Big changes that affect the organization, such as leadership changes, policy amendments or strategy shift, should be communicated in easy-to-understand language. People understand things in different ways and not everyone is comfortable with overly technical terms or language, for example. Use common language and tone that everyone can understand, therefore including them in the journey, mission and communication.

Employees must also accept that transparency at smaller organizations and at larger organizations are two very different things. It is a lot easier to communicate often when you are around 100 people. It's easy to speak frankly and honestly, with an understanding that there is likely quite a lot of group think and therefore a similar mindset of understanding your message. When you have numbers of employees closer to 1,000 and above, this is different. You will (or at least should) have a dedicated press team and internal communication team to finetune communications to ensure they are clear, appropriate and fair. Time with leaders should be spent understanding how to deliver difficult messages empathetically. Within reason, if you are sharing something at a company internal event, you should be comfortable with the fact it may leak. Otherwise, you put an onus on employees who may need to discuss things with their families etc to not do so, therefore making life decisions more difficult.

Open salary frameworks

This is self-explanatory. Everyone understands what everyone at every level is paid. There is no discrepancy between people. A Director is paid £X regardless of who they are. There is work to do to roll out an open salary framework as many people are uncomfortable with people understanding or knowing what they earn. Unfortunately, money and personal earnings is a heavily guarded topic that perpetuates exclusive practices. How can someone know if they are underpaid if they have no idea what their counterparts are paid?

If you do not have an open salary framework currently and want to have one, this will involve a substantial amount of work in communicating early why you want to do this and how. There may be people who are paid off framework (ie the amount they are paid is more than the framework says they should be for their level) and one-to-one meetings will need to happen with them to avoid any confusion or worry that they will be demoted. There'll need to be analysis to understand how many people are paid off framework and how to deal with these exceptions – they either permanently remain off framework but have salary rises in line with the framework or they can get promoted but do not have a salary increase until they are back in line with the expected salary for their level.

If you are starting out, this is a great opportunity to embed this early in the business. People will decide whether an open salary framework is a positive or negative for them and whether it's a driver to wanting to join or not join. For the most part, this is a positive.

Keep in mind that gender pay gap reporting is compulsory (and it is likely that ethnicity pay gap reporting will be compulsory in the near future). Having an open salary framework means that it is not possible for people to be paid differently for the same role. Where you may find your gap is in the distribution of underrepresented groups in senior leadership positions, which will be higher paid. Therefore if you pay everyone equally for roles but you do not have any women or people of colour in senior leadership roles, then you'll still have a gap. However, this is a different problem than pay inequity.

Code of conduct

Your code of conduct makes it very clear what is not acceptable in your workplace and should be aligned to your grievance process that allows people to raise their concerns if something breaks this conduct. Your code of conduct should also include any other useful information around what you expect from employees. This should be transparent and concise, yet still detailed enough to not be vague. A good code of conduct will cover physical and mental behaviours, calling out specific types of behaviour you will not tolerate such as sexism, racism, homophobia, transphobia, ableism etc. Be clear on:

- who the code of conduct is for;
- why you have one;
- what you require and ask of all employees;
- what happens when the code of conduct isn't followed or broken;
- any relevant contact details of your HR function.

A great example of a code of conduct is that of Black Girl Fest. Black Girl Fest is dedicated to amplifying the voices and experiences of Black British women and girls through community-based events. You can view their full code of conduct on their website (Black Girl Fest, 2019). Here are my favourite parts:

1 They clearly call out the different behaviours that are not acceptable, therefore providing no confusion about what will not be tolerated.

Offensive comments related to gender, gender identity and expression, sexual orientation, disability, mental illness, neurotype, physical appearance, body, age, race, ethnicity, nationality, language or religion. Unwelcome comments regarding a person's lifestyle choices and practices, including those related to food, health, parenting, drugs and employment.

Deliberate misgendering or use of 'dead' or rejected names.

Conversations or presentations that involve racism, ableism, misogyny.

2 They make it clear that they prioritize marginalized people's experiences and impacts over majority demographics, leaving no confusion that reverse -ism complaints, such as reverse racism or people being called out for perpetuating sexism etc, will not be acted on, at staff discretion.

Black Girl Festival prioritizes marginalized people's safety over privileged people's comfort. Festival staff reserve the right not to act on complaints regarding 'reverse' -isms, including 'reverse racism', 'reverse sexism' and 'cisphobia'.

3 Tone policing is proactively called out, therefore ensuring victims are prioritized over perpetuators taking issue with how victims communicate their upset.

Communicating in a 'tone' you don't find congenial.

Black Girls Fest's Code is focused on community events and this would need tweaking substantially for a corporate setting. Whilst all issues raised will need investigation from all sides, as per any corporate policy, this code of conduct is a good example of setting the tone on what is and isn't acceptable. It's important those hearing grievances are appropriately trained on 'reverse'-isms, to ensure these can be discussed and actioned properly. Many HR professionals are not equipped for these conversations, which can be deeply uncomfortable therefore causing more harm to those already affected.

Psychologically safe grievance process

A grievance process is the formal way for your employees to raise any issues or complaints about the workplace. This can be about the workplace itself or about a specific person. This process must work for all involved, creating a safe, transparent and clean-cut way for people to raise issues and have them investigated accordingly. There should be face-to-face and anonymous ways for employees to do this. You should have a system in place to do so anonymously and be able to succinctly state how it protects the employees' anonymity whilst still providing you with useful information on how to investigate any cases, if necessary.

Those who hear employees' grievances must be trained appropriately – they should not simply hear grievances because they are of a certain level of seniority in your organization. Similarly to interviewers, not everyone is suitable to have this responsibility and you must be prepared for that conversation. Training should cover how to deal with situations covering inappropriate behaviour, sexism, racism, physical/mental assault or abuse etc. There should be analysis done to understand the demographics (age, gender, ethnicity etc) of those listening to the grievances to unearth any affinity bias (that's the unconscious bias to get along with others who are like us). You should also analyse the overall percentages of cases with actionable vs non-actionable conclusions and then place an additional lens on this to understand the rate of actionable vs non-actionable conclusions when the issue is dealing with, for example, ethnicity-related grievances. Be clear on the repercussions of actioned grievances and breaking the code of conduct in work. There must be clear consequences of action.

Quite often, we see that the pool of HR Business Partners or 'People Partners' are primarily white women. Quite often we see white women viewed as the pinnacle of diversity (more on that later) and therefore an assumption is made that they are adequately trained to deal with *all* inclusion-related issues. Wrong. Consider an ethnicity-related grievance is raised and your HR Business Partner has no training or experience of dealing with ethnicity-related issues. What is the impact on the person who has raised this issue? A poor experience, lack of understanding and feeling emotionally exhausted from raising something painful with no reasonable outcome. This is relevant for many other issues too, not just ethnicity.

If the majority of this group is from a majority demographic, it will be worth doing surveys and listening sessions with under-represented employees to determine whether they are actually comfortable raising any marginalized issues, and if not, why not. If there are reasons why people are not comfortable raising issues, listen to them, discuss them and decide meaningful actions.

For me, inclusion means being proactive about ensuring people are purposefully listened to and potentially having the difficult conversations with those who are being exclusive. Now... what is privilege?

References

Anti-Defamation League (2020) [accessed 13 December 2020] Reports of Anti-Asian Assaults, Harassment and Hate Crimes Rise as Coronavirus Spreads [Online] www.adl.org/blog/reports-of-anti-asian-assaults-harassment-and-hate-crimes-rise-as-coronavirus-spreads (archived at https://perma.cc/469J-NV2P)

Bayern, M (2019) [accessed 13 December 2020] Why More Than Half of Women Leave the Tech Industry, *TechRepublic* [Online] www.techrepublic.com/article/why-more-than-half-of-women-leave-the-tech-industry/ (archived at https://perma.cc/DB7A-KD6W)

BBC News (2020) [accessed 13 December 2020] A-levels and GCSEs: How Did the Exam Algorithm Work? *BBC News*, 20 August [Online] www.bbc.co.uk/news/explainers-53807730 (archived at https://perma. cc/CNQ6-RVL4)

Bernal, N and Dodds, L (2019) [accessed 13 December 2020] 'Rosetta Stone' of AI Slammed for 'Racist' Classification of People's Faces, *The Telegraph*, 17 September [Online] www.telegraph.co.uk/technology/2019/09/17/ rosetta-stone-ai-slammed-racist-classification-peoples-faces/ (archived at https://perma.cc/8MQ7-2E2W)

Black Girl Fest (2019) [accessed 13 December 2020] Our Code of Conduct [Online] www.blackgirlfest.com (archived at https://perma.cc/ 54GD-3N59)

Buolamwini, J, Gebru, T, Friedler, S and Wilson, C (2018) [accessed 13 December 2020] Gender Shades: Intersectional Accuracy Disparities in Commercial Gender Classification, *Proceedings of Machine Learning Research*, 81, pp 1–15 [Online] http://proceedings.mlr.press/v81/ buolamwini18a/buolamwini18a.pdf (archived at https://perma.cc/ 2FBT-522Q)

Catalyst (2018) [accessed 13 December 2020] Too Few Women of Color on Boards: Statistics and Solutions [Online] www.catalyst.org/research/ women-minorities-corporate-boards (archived at https://perma.cc/ 922T-LB87)

Cook, J (2019) [accessed 13 December 2020] 'Racist' Passport Photo System Rejects Image of a Young Black Man Despite Meeting Government Standards, *The Telegraph*, 19 September [Online] www.telegraph.co.uk/ technology/2019/09/19/racist-passport-photo-system-rejects-image-young-black-man-despite/ (archived at https://perma.cc/J39J-DYCJ)

Doherty, F (2019) [accessed 13 December 2020] Is Your Recruitment Process a Help or Hinderance to Social Mobility? [Online] https:// groupgti.com/insights/is-your-recruitment-process-a-help-or-hinderance-to-social-mobility (archived at https://perma.cc/7LM6-9LWE)

Gov England, Wales and Scotland (2019) [accessed 13 December 2020] Employment, Service.gov.uk [Online] www.ethnicity-facts-figures. service.gov.uk/work-pay-and-benefits/employment/employment/latest (archived at https://perma.cc/P4X4-NS4R)

Hunt, V, Layton, D and Prince, S (2015) [accessed 13 December 2020] Why Diversity Matters, *McKinsey* [Online] www.mckinsey.com/ business-functions/organization/our-insights/why-diversity-matters# (archived at https://perma.cc/7CAY-X2AZ)

Inclusive Boards (2019) [accessed 13 December 2020] Disability in Senior Leadership Toolkit [Online] www.inclusionbarnet.org.uk/wp-content/ uploads/2019/09/Disability-in-Senior-Leadership-Toolkit-by-Inclusive-Boards.pdf (archived at https://perma.cc/PK3P-P6F4)

Kelly, C (2020) [accessed 13 December 2020] Two Black Transgender Women Were Killed Last Week, Thousands Showed Up to Protest, *USA TODAY* [Online] https://eu.usatoday.com/story/news/nation/2020/06/15/ deaths-black-trans-women-riah-milton-dominique-fells-spur-protests/ 3191769001/ (archived at https://perma.cc/9A6R-9ATC)

LGBT Map (2018) [accessed 13 December 2020] The Legal Landscape for LGBT Workers [Online] www.lgbtmap.org/file/LGBT-Workers-3-Pager-FINAL.pdf (archived at https://perma.cc/6Q44-WSAR)

McMillan, G (2011) [accessed 13 December 2020] It's Not You, It's It: Voice Recognition Doesn't Recognize Women, *Time* [Online] https:// techland.time.com/2011/06/01/its-not-you-its-it-voice-recognition-doesnt-recognize-women/ (archived at https://perma.cc/4EEY-5TVQ)

Scope (2019) [accessed 13 December 2020] Disability Price Tag [Online] www.scope.org.uk/campaigns/extra-costs/disability-price-tag/ (archived at https://perma.cc/TNV2-RKFF)

Stonewall (2018) [accessed 13 December 2020] Stonewall Reveals Coming out at Work Still a Problem [Online] www.stonewall.org.uk/ about-us/media-centre/media-statement/stonewall-reveals-coming-out-work-still-problem (archived at https://perma.cc/MW9V-9AAZ)

Transport for London (2020) [accessed 13 December 2020] Step-Free Access [Online] https://tfl.gov.uk/travel-information/improvements-and-projects/step-free-access#:~:text=Currently%2079%20Tube%20 stations%2C%2060 (archived at https://perma.cc/73W2-LJHA)

Turvill, W (2019) [accessed 13 December 2020] Taking the Mickey: Men Called Michael Outnumber Women Chairing FTSE Firms, *This is Money* [Online] www.thisismoney.co.uk/money/markets/ article-7414653/Men-called-Michael-outnumber-women-chairing-FTSE-firms.html (archived at https://perma.cc/H3A8-JP73)

Wagner, L (2019) [accessed 13 December 2020] Disabled People in the World in 2019: Facts and Figures [Online] www.inclusivecitymaker. com/disabled-people-in-the-world-in-2019-facts-and-figures (archived at https://perma.cc/TW5D-RVPV)

Welson-Rossman, T (2020) [accessed 13 December 2020] New Capital One Survey Shows How Companies Can Retain More Female Technologists, *Forbes* [Online] www.forbes.com/sites/traceywelsonrossman/2019/10/01/ new-capital-one-survey-shows-how-companies-can-retain-more-female-technologists/?sh=698379b16076 (archived at https://perma.cc/AQC3-XEZ2)

World Economic Forum (2020) [accessed 13 December 2020] The Coronavirus Fallout May be Worse for Women Than Men. Here's Why [Online] www.weforum.org/agenda/2020/03/the-coronavirus-fallout-may-be-worse-for-women-than-men-heres-why/ (archived at https:// perma.cc/8CCY-D94E)

CHAPTER THREE

Privilege

The haves and the have nots

This chapter will focus on:

- What is privilege?
- Why does it make people uncomfortable?
- How has privilege made things easier for some and harder for others?
- What is intersectionality?
- What can we do?

What is privilege?

For me, privilege is a set of unearned benefits given to people who fit into a specific social group – there is no skill to being privileged. There is a lot to unpack in this and we will go on that journey in this chapter.

The word 'privilege' is becoming more commonplace – it is being said and heard more often. Some become defensive at the mention of the word, without truly understanding what it means and how it affects those who were not afforded the same unearned benefits. To truly understand how to support, empower and retain those from minority backgrounds, businesses and the people who work within them must acknowledge how society has benefited the majority.

Firstly, what is a 'right'? What are we given a right to and why? What do you believe is your given right? And why is that? Do you think people's views on rights differ across groups like gender, race, class, sexual orientation, disability or any other characteristic?

Rights are things that should be given to all people, regardless of the above. Can you say that what you view as a right is a right for everyone else? For me, I deserve the right to vote, to have basic necessities, to go where I want and need to go, to body autonomy, to be able to walk late at night and feel safe, to be able to be in a relationship with whomever I want to be with and to not be judged negatively on my skin colour. However, it is highly unlikely I have all of these things – I certainly have many more of these rights now that I am financially secure and stable.

An example that is close to me is Northern Ireland, where I am from. Due to the government voting in Northern Ireland, women do not have body autonomy and only in 2019 was gay marriage allowed legally. This may not affect you (or even me) but it's important to remember that no one deserves or earned these rights over anyone else. The world is made from the lenses of the majority, and as we have seen before, the majority are those in powerful positions, shaping what the world of tomorrow looks like.

But where does that leave those who aren't at those tables, or are at the tables, but are not being heard?

Why does it make people uncomfortable and how has privilege made things easier for some and harder for others?

Let's think about what 'unearned benefits' actually means. 'Unearned' means there is no skill to achieving these things, you simply either have them or you don't. It is luck, not skill or talent. That can be a difficult thing to take in if privilege has benefited you in your life. We may work hard, but that doesn't mean there aren't things that could have made our lives harder – and that these things do actively make other people's lives harder. Let's go through some examples.

We hear about 'male privilege' often, and we are going to talk about that here too (and more). Let's start with this example as many will be aware of it, whether you agree with it or not.

Male privilege is the system of advantages or rights that are available to men solely on the basis of their sex. A man's access to these benefits may vary depending on how closely they match their society's ideal masculine norm. It is really important that we remember the lens of 'ideal masculine norm', what that is and why society places so much importance on it. Ninety-eight per cent of CEOs in S&P companies and 95.1 per cent of Fortune CEOs are men (*Harvard Business Review*, 2019). When we talk about male privilege at work, the ability to succeed because success is an attribute that people readily expect of you is a very real element. What this means is that processes are made in a way that considers you – therefore meaning you absolutely do not need to consider them.

When we talk about the privilege of being a man, this is because stereotypes play into what 'being a man is'. Society has so readily rewarded men for being physically strong, heterosexual, high financial earners and unbothered with emotion – whilst so easily penalized those who are not. These stereotypes either work in your favour or they do not. When women typically try to embody these traits, they are not deemed attractive or influential, rather bossy and catty, which then creates an unattainable goal to success.

One element of male privilege and abiding by society's ideal masculine norm is safety. Do you worry about walking home late at night, or being alone in a country that is new to you? Do you worry about being attacked and having no chance of fighting off someone? Do you worry about being in a relationship with someone and being at a higher risk of domestic abuse (Womens Aid, 2019)?

Another area of male privilege is childcare responsibilities. Having children forms a part of the majority of people's lives, whether it's by choice, biologically, fostering, adoption or other means. When a child has two parents, in an ideal world responsibilities would be split evenly; however, that is not the case. It is important to understand the impact of this and what has brought us to this place. I mentioned previously that men are more likely to be in higher-paying roles. One of the side effects of the preference and positive bias towards men in leadership means that, predominantly, women stay at home and look after children. This comes from the societal norms around marriage, bearing children and caring for them. Realistically, if women were in similar higher-paying roles, would this responsibility be so heavily skewed? I personally don't think so. There is also a huge pressure on women to be 'mothers', whether they want children or not. And the same pressure does not exist for men. Again, these pressures and problems add up to an existence of very real privilege.

If you are a man, you don't have these problems. That is not to say you don't have problems at all – it just means you don't have *these* problems.

Here is another example of class and race privilege.

Society places a huge importance on where you are from, whether you attended school or not (and if you did, what school you did attend). You have no choice in the matter as to where you are born or adopted to (depending on age). It is ordinarily entirely out of your control, yet it definitively shapes your life, what your opportunities may be and how easy it is for you to reach the goals you may have. In 2013, a study by Harvard economist and author Nathaniel Hendren showed that your potential for climbing the income ladder in the United States is largely dependent on your hometown (Leonhardt, 2013). 'Where you grow up matters, there is tremendous variation across the US in the extent to which kids can rise out of poverty' (Moyers, 2013). Depending on your postal code, it is likely you may never rise out of poverty. This is also prevalent in the UK. Things entirely out of our control either give or remove privilege.

When we understand that backgrounds and namely poverty play a huge role in our opportunities, we also need to understand how poverty disproportionately affects those from ethnic minority backgrounds than those who are white. This conversation cannot be had without talking about slavery and the impact of poverty on Black people. In 1940, in the United States, 60 per cent of employed Black women worked as domestic servants. In 1998, this number was down to 2.2 per cent, while 60 per cent held white-collar jobs. In 1958, 44 per cent of whites said they would move if a Black family became their next door neighbour. In 1998, this figure was 1 per cent. These are not statistics, but rather people's grandparents, parents, relatives, and likely people who are still alive. The impact of slavery means that Black people are disproportionately represented in lower-paid roles and underrepresented roles. Yet again, undeserved and unearned societal-deemed disadvantages creating a chasm that cannot be easily bridged through hard work, luck and determination.

If we think about how your postcode defines the type of school that you can attend, alongside the type of work you are exposed to, it's no surprise that Black people are particularly underrepresented in the workforce. If you never had to fight against the impact of your ancestors being forcibly displaced, stolen and made into slaves, then you don't and cannot possibly understand facing these same barriers.

Class barriers are a very real thing. Let's consider how people view accents.

Think about someone you view as successful. What do they sound like? Do they sound like the people you see portrayed as successful in TV shows or something different? One very real element of privilege is the association of intelligence to an accent. This is something I feel very close to me, as someone with a thick Irish accent, working in leadership roles where there are primarily only people from London represented. Slang and different ways of saying things are looked at differently and create another barrier to success, regardless of the content of what you're saying.

These associations change and directly affect how people view us and our lives, especially in the workplace. Several studies have shown there is an 'accent hierarchy' and as part of the Accent Bias In Britain project, researchers at Queen Mary University of London and University of York examined public attitudes to accent 'labels' and responses to recorded voices, before looking more specifically at how accent bias plays out in professional settings (Accent Bias Britain, 2019). Their research showed that there is still a very clear accent hierarchy that clearly disadvantages 'non-standard working-class and ethnic accents and upholds the belief that national standard varieties are the most prestigious'. This isn't limited to the UK – it's global. For those working in the United States, research has shown that those with non-standard accents face disadvantages in pay, gain less fundraising and are less likely to be promoted up the business ranks (Huang, 2020). Yet again, another undeserved, unearned benefit if this is something you do not worry about.

One thing I deliver in industry is privilege awareness training. This covers how bias has shaped society, what this means for our day-to-day in work and at home and some exercises that help people understand privilege in a more nuanced and personal way. One of these exercises is called a privilege walk. You will likely have seen this in practice before as it is a widely used exercise in inclusion-related training and discussions. Originally created by Peggy McIntosh to discuss 'unpacking the invisible knapsack', its goal is to open up the conversation on privilege and the importance of this in everyday life (Andersson, 2014). In this exercise, participants all start at the same line/number and depending on how they answer, they move back or forwards. It by no means covers every single element of privilege, but it does open up a conversation and help folks engage with something that might be very uncomfortable.

What is intersectionality?

This exercise may seem very long as you read it (it takes approximately 45 minutes to run in person); however, I haven't shortened it for a number of reasons. Privilege is incredibly intricate and it is a layered experience. How you are treated is never isolated down to one characteristic. This is called intersectionality and we'll talk more about this later. The privilege walk is pretty long because it covers lots of different areas – gender, ethnicity, disability, neurodiversity, sexual orientation, economic background, language, nationality and more. The culmination of all of these different traits deems how society treats and values you and none is any more or less important than the other. Each deserves the time to discuss and understand.

I'm going to share these questions here (answer along and count your score – you start at 0) and explain a little beside each question as to why it is asked and its importance.

Privilege walk exercise

1 If you are white, step forward.
2 If you are a person of colour, step back.
   White privilege is a very real thing. We've spoken about a few small examples above and it's important we realize that being white, even if you are poor, a member of the LGBT+ community, disabled etc still means that one thing that doesn't make your life harder is your skin colour. Racism is more than calling someone a racial slur – it is subtle.
3 If you are a man, step forward.
4 If you didn't step forward for point 3, step back.
   We have previously discussed male privilege. It includes the security of knowing success is attributed to your gender, the potential less worry around personal safety, and the stereotypes that play into your favour because of gender norms.
5 If you identify with the gender you were assigned at birth, step forward.
6 If you didn't step forward for point 5, step back.
   This means you are comfortable and happy with the gender you were assigned at birth. Transgender folks do not have that privilege and it's important that if you have not had to worry, you consider the serious emotional, psychological and physical health impact, alongside potential financial costs to transitioning. There is a lot to understand if you are cisgendered (that means you identify with the gender you were assigned at birth!).

In 2018, HRC tracked at least 26 deaths of transgender or gender non-conforming people in the United States due to fatal violence (Human Rights Campaign, 2018). The large majority of these women were Black. They were killed by acquaintances, partners and strangers – many who have not been caught, arrested or charged. There are times where these cases involve clear anti-transgender bias; however, there were other times when the victim's transgender status may have been putting them at risk, meaning they were forced into homelessness, unsafe environments, poverty and/or survival sex work.

7 If you are heterosexual, step forward.

8 If you didn't step forward for point 7, step back.

If you are not a member of the LGBTQA+ (that's lesbian, gay, bisexual, transgender, queer or asexual+) community, you will not have had to consider whether your sexual orientation or gender conformity will put you at risk – whether that's risk of livelihood, safety, financial stability, opportunity and more. I worked in consulting for many years creating LGBTQA+ inclusion strategies, and one of the most prevalent issues raised was in the environment where folks change projects, teams and managers regularly, so they have to make a personal decision (that may mean they are treated differently due to conscious, unconscious or unchecked homophobia) whether to 'come out' each time this happened.

Simply existing shouldn't put your livelihood and safety at risk, but for many folks it does.

9 If you are under 40, step forward.

The reason this is included is that it's important to understand there is usually a flexibility allowed for being younger – potentially fewer life commitments, ability to take more risks and more. This is, of course, not a blanket statement, but overarchingly it makes a difference. Additionally, there are some health changes that are especially prevalent in older folks, such as menopause, that require different support, both mentally and physically.

10 If you are a member of one or more other underrepresented groups, take a step back for each one.

Privilege is layered and intricate. These things all add up and cause different effects. This is called intersectionality. This theory was developed by Kimberlé Williams Crenshaw, a US lawyer, civil rights advocate, philosopher and a leading scholar of critical race theory. We will talk about this in more depth soon!

11 If you have visible or invisible disabilities, step back.

12 If you have ever been unable to attend a meeting or event space because a lift was out of order or there was no appropriate access, step back.

13 If you ever had to ask for a seat on public transport, step back.

14 If you ever had to turn on an accessibility feature on your phone in order to use an app, step back.

Disabilities are not always visibly obvious. Disability affects many people in many, many different ways. There is potentially an extra physical, mental, emotional and financial cost to being disabled. In the UK, we have the National Health Service that aims to provide free healthcare for all, funded by taxpayers; however, in the United States or other countries without healthcare support, this does not exist. Additionally, UK wait times are lengthy.

For example, if you use a wheelchair, you may constantly worry about whether there will be appropriate access/door widths for you to get to events/hotels/homes. If you have a chronic illness, such as endometriosis, you may have extra worries about searching for jobs that can support the different rest periods that you may need. There are many more lenses to this too, and we will discuss these in more detail later.

If you are non-disabled, these are not things you have to consider.

15 If you have a university degree, step forward.

16 If you attended an elite university, step forward.

17 If you owe student loans, step back.

Attending university in itself is a privilege. It is expensive and not everyone has been exposed to university possibly due to upbringing, cultural influences and family responsibilities. I attended university, but I am now plagued with debt because of it. I was also 'lucky' enough to hit a low-family-household income threshold that meant I was able to get a little bursary.

It is also important to note the association of 'intelligence' to certain universities and the snobbery that exists around people attending or not attending those. Russell Group (the Russell Group is a self-selected association of 24 public research universities in the UK) and elite universities across the globe create different levels of 'credibility' regardless of the educational content.

I want us to think of the barriers to accessing those kinds of universities. There are steep fees but even steeper cultural and economic association barriers. For example, at Cambridge University, just 39 Black students enrolled in 2016. Nevertheless, this figure was a record high, up from 38 and 35 in 2015 and 2014. In total, 2,622 students from the UK accepted undergraduate places at Cambridge in 2016 (Menin and Ashworth, 2017). What's important to note here is that this is the first time Cambridge University has accepted more Black students than students from Eton, which is one of the UK's most prestigious private schools.

An investigation by Varsity found in 2016 that only 12.9 per cent of Black applicants accepted a place at Cambridge University. In contrast, 28.1 per cent of white applicants took up a place, while the overall average was 26.4 per cent (Menin and Ashworth, 2017). These numbers do not shock me. There is an overwhelming clear association of those who can reach and be accepted into these universities – they are from white, financially privileged backgrounds.

There have been many discussions about the percentage of UK Prime Ministers that have attended these universities and Eton. Out of 55 Prime Ministers, 20 attended Eton, 28 attended Oxford and 14 attended Cambridge. This raises the point around the barrier to attend but also the association of money, power, credibility and intelligence to attend in the first place, therefore deeming other universities to be lesser.

18 If you are now financially able to take unpaid leave, step forward.

In a similar thread to university, financial stability and safety are privileges and if you are working, being able to take unpaid leave is a good measure of that. There are several questions here because it is likely many of our financial securities will change throughout our lives, in peaks and troughs.

If you have always been able to take unpaid leave, it's likely you are from a higher economic background that has allowed you financial stability either at the start of or before your own earning role. And if you can take it now, you are likely in a role that provides a salary that allows you to take days off with no money. Not everyone has these privileges and we should recognize that.

For context, Oxfam has studies that show the very top of the economic pyramid sees trillions of dollars of wealth in the hands of a very small group of people, predominantly men, whose fortune and power grow exponentially. Billionaires have now more wealth than the 4.6 billion people who make up 60 per cent of the planet's population (Oxfam, 2019).

19 If you have always been financially able to take unpaid leave, step forward.

20 If you didn't step forward for point 19, step back.

21 If you are concerned about losing your job because of your financial situation, step back.

22 If you haven't been able to join in out-of-office lunches or after-work social activities because of the cost, step back.

23 If English is your first language, step forward.

24 If your location has a regional language typically used and you do not speak it fluently/comfortably, step back.

25 If you have a different accent from the majority where you work, step back.

26 If you are from an area outside the main city in your country, with a different regional accent, step back.

Language and accent are interesting discussions. About 360 million people speak English as their first language, which is around 20 per cent. This doesn't seem like a massive amount, right? Yet, the English language dominates business rooms and more. Realistically, this is because of the colonization of the world by Great Britain, therefore elevating the language they brought with them.

Accents play a huge role in how 'important' and 'intelligent' we deem people to be, too. Accent Bias Britain, an organization dedicated to this very topic, has shared a lot of insight on this. In their latest report, the UK public has shown remarkable consistency over the past 50 years. Their results confirm that labels such as 'Queen's English' and 'Own English' fare well, and that certain local (eg 'Birmingham') and ethnic (eg 'Afro-Caribbean') accent labels fare poorly.

There is some evidence that differences between accents are reducing: while standard accents are still ranked highest and urban and ethnic vernaculars ranked lowest, the quantitative distances between the top- and bottom-rated accents are smaller in our study than in either 2004 or 1969.

Nevertheless, the results show a persistent hierarchy of accent evaluations, one that penalizes non-standard working-class and ethnic accents and upholds the belief that national standard varieties are the most prestigious. (Accent Bias Britain, 2019)

Additionally, language in itself is a unique barrier. I've done this exercise globally and, especially in certain European regions, this is noticeable. For example, in the Nordics, all legislation is written in Norwegian, so if you don't speak/ write Norwegian, clients won't work with you. In various different regions of Belgium, people speak French, in others they speak Flemish and in others German, and again, if you don't speak the right language in the right place, getting jobs (and high paid jobs especially) is incredibly difficult. Consider the impact of this for those who are either 1) from poorer backgrounds and potentially haven't been taught two languages or 2) immigrants who move to a country.

There is a lot to understand in how we are able to be proud of a country's heritage and language without being actively exclusionary to those who potentially don't speak our language(s) or identify entirely with all aspects of our culture.

27　If your company sponsors your work visa, step back.

If your company sponsors your work visa, your rights to remain in the place you live are dependent on your employer. That can create difficult attachments when it comes to potentially wanting to leave toxic, negative workplaces, but not being able to due to this need to stay. Immigration processes are expensive and lengthy – many folks cannot afford these alone.

28　If you have a name that is expected in the country where you work, step forward.

29　If your name is regularly spelled incorrectly or mispronounced, step back.

30　If you are regularly mistaken as someone else of the same ethnicity, step back.

31　If you didn't step back for point 30, step forward.

How important is your name to you? What does it signify? Is it yours and only yours? Even if someone else has the same name, your name is still singularly belonging to your personality.

Names in environments where they are not common are seen as 'outliers' and 'different'. That, in itself, defines you as 'the other'. Let's consider the United States and the UK, where some of the most popular names are Oliver, Harry,

Eva, Liam and Isabella – common, Western names. Most folks don't struggle to pronounce these names. But what about names that are not Westernized – like Nirushika, Tunde and more?

It is important to remember the associate of 'success' that we talked about before. White people, and white men, are more represented in leadership than any other demographics. Their names are typically well understood, and due to their power, if there is effort needed to be expended to say their names, that will happen.

In countries, like the UK, where Black, Asian or ethnic minority people make up around 14 per cent of the country, there is a bias against names that are not deemed belonging of the other 86 per cent. People from these backgrounds progressing into the workforce and leadership positions means there are biases playing against them as 1) people similar to them do not make that jump as often as white people do and 2) because there are fewer people like them already at decision-making tables, the processes and ways of working that already exist have not been created with their needs in consideration.

In addition to all of this, people regularly saying your name wrong, especially after they have been corrected, is disrespectful. I think about this a lot, as a woman of colour who was almost named Nirushika Atcheson instead of Sheree Atcheson. My name and Irish accent give me an anonymity that means no one can tell I am a person of colour until they see me – therefore, for example in CV screening or on phone calls, I do not face the same bias as other people of colour do.

Why being mistaken for someone of the same ethnicity is offensive should be easy to understand. It is boiling someone down to their ethnicity only – disregarding their personality, who they are, their impact and more. It has happened to me in the past and it is jarring and upsetting. I know this directly *affects Black and brown people more than white folks too. You may remember when Kobe Bryant passed away in 2020 and BBC news ran a memoriam to him, whilst using photos of LeBron James, or when Dawn Butler Brent, a Labour MP, was confused for fellow MP Marsha de Cordova whilst saying this happens to her regularly.*

If this doesn't happen to you, please consider what this feels like. And intervene when you can.

32 If you have ever felt passed over for a job based on your gender, ethnicity, age or sexual orientation, step back.

33 If you have ever felt excluded from key social or networking opportunities because of your gender, ethnicity, age or sexual orientation, step back.

34 If you have been asked to do menial and admin-related office tasks that colleagues of another gender are not asked to do, step back.

35 If you have been removed from a project because a client was concerned about your gender, ethnicity, age or sexual orientation, step back.

36 If you have recently received feedback about a technical skill you need to learn, step forward.

37 If you have been told to wait your turn for a promotion or exciting project assignment behind a similarly qualified peer, step back.

We've spoken about these biases above. Remember that biases don't exist in isolation, they affect everything – including who gets what job and why, who is left out of social events because they may be different and who is assigned the 'office glue work' that is integral to things happening, but so readily is forgotten in promotion cases. A few examples of this are note taking, actively mentoring other more junior team members or spending the time sharing knowledge across the team.

There is an important part here in how feedback is crucial to getting ahead in any environment. How can you know what you do well and can do better if no one tells you? Studies have shown that white women and women of colour with white men managers typically do not receive the technical feedback they need to progress, but receive feedback focusing more on their 'human-skills', which you may call soft skills. These are important, but it is almost impossible to progress without some technical understanding for your work. And if you are not getting that, then you're not getting the same runway to progress as those who do receive constructive, detailed feedback.

38 If you can speak openly about your significant other(s), step forward.

This is specifically focusing on those from the LGBTQA+ community and those from religious backgrounds who may not feel able to talk about their partner.

We can use more inclusive language around how we talk about our own partners (if we're cisgendered and heterosexual) by using gender-neutral terms, such as 'partner' or 'spouse', instead of 'boyfriend', 'girlfriend', 'husband' or 'wife'.

39 If someone else has assumed you were a lower seniority level than you are, step back.

40 If you feel you can actively and effectively contribute to meetings you attend, step forward.

41 If you are regularly interrupted or ignored in meetings when others are not, step back.

Seniority level is important in privilege. Being more senior usually means having the privilege of being listened to and, at a minimum, having access to the rooms you need to do your job effectively.

However, there is a difference in speaking, and speaking and being heard. I'm sure you'll all have experienced this in your lives. We can all speak verbally, or in whatever mode of communication we choose, but if no one listens or actions what you're communicating, how do you feel? Disengaged and unimportant. Likewise, being interrupted regularly can be a sign of disrespect or being viewed as not important enough to warrant being listened to. It is crucial we spend time actually thinking about who we listen to and why. Are we actively zoning out other voices subconsciously or consciously?

I spend a lot of my time training leaders to make sure they are not just providing avenues for their people to speak but also actionable outcomes based on what they are hearing – even if it's difficult and uncomfortable.

42 If your manager avoids eye contact when speaking to you, step back.

43 If you are comfortable making eye contact in meetings, step forward.

We make eye contact usually with those we have a connection to.

If you are 'the only', this can be difficult. Studies have shown that men managers at times are more likely to make more eye contact with workers they see as high performers and avoid eye contact with workers they see as lower status. Let's remember that underrepresented people are typically in junior and mid-tier roles in work. You see the connections I'm making here? If we only make eye-contact with those in higher status roles, and most of the people in those roles are white, non-disabled, financially stable men, then we are making the subconscious connection that everyone else is lesser.

The flipside of this is remembering how neurodiversity can play into this. The term neurodiversity refers to variation in the human brain regarding sociability, learning, attention, mood and other mental functions in a non-pathological sense. This means people who are, for example, autistic, have dyslexia or dyspraxia etc. Eye-contact for neurodiverse people can be incredibly difficult and uncomfortable, so it is important we think about this and amend our conversation styles and ways of communication. We should be trying to support people of all different needs in the best ways we can.

44 If you are the primary caregiver for someone, step back.

45 If you have a partner who takes on a large share of household and family responsibilities, step forward.

46 If you are financially supporting a parent, grandparent or sibling, step back.

Looking after someone is not easy. Whether that is children, parents, siblings, relatives, friends or anyone else. It takes time, money, physical, emotional and mental strength and so many folks do it on top of salaried jobs (when this is a job in itself).

Consider the cultural impact here too. In many communities, such as Black and Asian communities, it is commonplace that those bringing in a wage look after the rest of the family. It is also common in families from poorer backgrounds (remember poverty also disproportionately affects brown and Black people more than white too).

This means that when we talk about expendable income and caring responsibilities, we must remember that there are different cultural elements at play. Not every person of X age on Y salary has Z extra money – it may be going to look after many different people.

If you have someone to help you, that's a privilege.

47 If you are the first in your family to attend university, step back.

48 If you were on free school meals at school (or equivalent), step back.

49 If you are from a lower socioeconomic background, step back.

Coming from a lower socioeconomic background and progressing is not easy. Being from a poorer background gives a different approach and set of barriers to life. There are different contexts in which people are raised too, which mean that there are different views of what success are and how you achieve that. Is it becoming a CEO or is it being able to have food on the table each night?

It's also harder to progress into spaces that are dominated by those from high economic backgrounds because you start feeling like you are 'the other' if you are the only one with a different background, from a different place, with a different accent and more. There are many unspoken knowledge pieces that those in more financial stable backgrounds have – how to negotiate, 'carrying yourself', how to be confident. These things do not always map over.

50 If you have ever been called a 'diversity hire', step back.

51 If you work in technology, have ever met someone at a technical meetup who assumed you must be the partner of someone technical, or that you work in a non-technical role, step back. (If you do not work in technology, skip this question).

52 If you have ever been mistaken for a member of the catering staff at an event, step back.

Being reduced to a 'diversity hire' is belittling, yet it happens often to underrepresented people. A 'diversity hire' is someone who has been hired just to look better from a diversity point of view – so likely a white woman, a person of colour or someone who is disabled.

Stereotypes are rampant in society, which means they are rampant in work if they are not challenged. Let's use an example – there are statistically less women in technology than we'd expect – with a peak of around 30 per cent being seen (in the good places) globally. Most organizations are hitting around 14–20 per cent. A common thing that happens at tech events is women in tech roles, such as engineering, are regularly asked if they are recruiters, in hiring or people-related roles. There is nothing bad about those roles (I do one of them!), but there is something wrong with assuming someone does a certain role just because they are under-represented in the field you are thinking of.

53 If you have ever received an unwanted sexual advance at work, step back.

54 If you have ever been harassed at work and changed teams or companies because of it, step back.

55 If you have ever felt unsafe at work or at a professional event, step back.

56 If you have ever felt unsafe leaving work late at night, or going home after an evening event, step back.

We have talked about this previously in detail and from a gender perspective. Feeling safe is a privilege that many folks do not need to worry about.

I also want to drill into the race and ethnicity element.

I want you to think about if you feel safe in your own home. When you sit down or go to sleep, do you feel safe and secure? Do you worry?

Are you Black? All Black folks may not worry about this (and that may be linked to how financially secure they feel, which could be reflected in where they live); however, I hope you remember this story:

On 6 September 2018, off-duty Dallas Police Department patrol officer Amber Guyger entered the Dallas, Texas, apartment of Botham Jean and fatally shot him. Guyger broke into Jean's home, pulled her weapon and shot him, in his own home. He was not out of the house. This story was seen globally and there was an outrage for the treatment of Jean's name and Guyger's preferential treatment from being both a white woman and a patrol officer – giving a cross-section of white feminism and power. We will talk about this intersection later. She received a 10-year sentence for murder (five years non-parole), whilst also receiving bizarre treatment with the judge giving her a hug and a Bible (Mervosh and Bogel-Burroughs, 2019). This treatment was called out by many because it doesn't align with how other non-white women have been treated when charged with similar (or lesser) crimes. The treatment in itself was scrutinized for many weeks afterwards.

Safety is an immense, regularly unspoken, privilege – it is a gateway to confidence and self-assuredness.

We have covered lots of different types of privilege here, and there are more! If you were completing this exercise, what is your score?

Mine is –11. As a young woman of colour raised in a very white space, now in a senior position in an overly white male-dominated industry, I am very underrepresented. However, I am also a heterosexual, cisgender, financially stable woman who can comfortably talk about her spouse. Privilege is nuanced and intricate.

I have run these workshops globally and usually there is a relatively clear breakdown in terms of gender and ethnicity. From back to front, usually there are:

- Black women;
- other women of colour and Black men;
- white women with caring responsibilities and other men of colour;
- white women with no caring responsibilities and white men with caring responsibilities;
- white men with no caring responsibilities.

This is just an overall view; it is not the way things always end up, but it's important to note that these trends happen. Spend some time thinking about your score, share this exercise with your friends, family and work colleagues. Think about how your life would be different if you stepped forward or back.

What can we do?

The aim of this exercise is to create more of an awareness of our own personal privilege. But what are you going to do with this awareness? We are at a stage in society where quietly agreeing is simply not good enough. We must stand up, be clear on what we're trying to achieve and use our privilege for those who do not have it. It's not good enough to, for example, quietly believe that Black people do not deserve to be brutalized at the hands of the police. If you are silent, you are leaning on a privilege to not openly engage.

We will talk more about allyship in detail later, but let's talk about ways to continually have this awareness of privilege after you set down this book.

Follow a diverse group of voices

We cannot understand or know all experiences singularly. One way to help diversify our knowledge is to follow people from both the same and different backgrounds to you. Twitter or LinkedIn is a great way to do this. You get an insight that you'll otherwise never have and it's a curated feed. I make a point of reviewing who I follow every few months and noting if there seems to be some imbalance. There are some tools out there that can analyse your following trends across gender (please keep in mind they only appear to work for binary people, therefore don't consider non-binary people etc).

Do this exercise at different points in your life

Privilege is not static – it changes with your life. Personally, my 'score' in the exercise above would have been much lower even just three years ago, and in the last six months it will have increased due to the seniority of roles I hold and the confidence that comes from that. It's important to recognize that as we evolve, things change. The Covid-19 pandemic is an example of this. During this period, there were many people who became caregivers who simply didn't have that responsibility before, parents who had to balance full-time caring responsibilities with work and people dealing with being furloughed or made redundant.

Consider what media you engage with and what you don't

Privilege gives us an ability to disengage with things we view as uncomfortable, irrelevant or unpalatable to us. Consider the groups of people that do not have that privilege. Do you genuinely show up for them if you do not engage with their stories, their history, their pain and their wins? The answer is no. Some ways to do this are to:

1 Make sure you keep up to date on what's happening in the world from a variety of news sources to try to counteract any media bias.
2 Watch shows and documentaries made about underrepresented people's stories and lives. Some of them will be painful, but please remember if it's painful for you, how painful is it for them? There are stories I have watched where I simply didn't know about them previously because of my privilege and it is eye opening – we must listen and learn.
3 Go to events that are typically about showcasing underrepresented people. Do you go to Black History Month events, or International Women's Day or Pride? If not, why not? Attending gives you an opportunity to learn about these experiences and widen your perspectives. This is a small show of allyship.

Take the time to understand how your privilege benefits you and disadvantages others

This is a continuous journey and not one you do overnight. It's hard but worthwhile.

I'll share a little more about my personal life here. I am a heterosexual woman of colour, married to a heterosexual white man. He is my partner in every sense of the word and I love him dearly. It would be silly to not engage with the fact we are an interracial couple from Northern Ireland. Back in Northern Ireland, there are not many couples like us, and it is still very obvious where we are from. Almost all family events will be a sea of white people (as you'd expect), which creates an unintended exclusive experience for me. We have to talk about how he is a white man and how he has an immense amount of privilege. He is from a poorer economic background and that has greatly affected his life, but by walking down the street, you cannot tell that. He still carries the privilege of being white and being a man.

We have had conversations about what we both do to be actionable allies and work to support people less privileged than us. For me, as a global leader in diversity, equity and inclusion (DE&I), I find it very easy to talk about what I need to do. He does not feel the same comfort and is on his own journey. We've spent time talking about what allyship means to him as a heterosexual white man. The main takeaway of these conversations is that he has to be willing to put himself out of his comfort zone and to go further than just agreeing that inequity is wrong. He must put his privilege on the line, openly and transparently.

To discuss privilege in depth from a different perspective, I sat down with Andy Ayim. Andy is the founder of The Angel Investing School (a school and community that provides professionals with live online classes on how to get started with investing in start-ups). He also consults with organizations on how to build Product teams that work with agility to create products customers love using his Product Playbooks. He was the Managing Director of Backstage Capital (a globally renowned venture capital and private equity fund that invests in the best startups globally, led by underrepresented founders) and has worked in a range of product roles in companies such as Investec Bank and WorldFirst, acquired by Ant Financial for US $700 million. Andy has dedicated his career to changing the ecosystem in the venture capital world, which notably is very homogeneous. Black founders lead only 1 per cent of VC backed startups. And 80 per cent of VC funds don't even have a single Black investor (Heller, 2020).

As someone who has dedicated their career to proactively helping underrepresented people, I asked Andy what drove him to do this personally – was it his own personal experiences as a Black man or was there a moment when he knew he had to do something? He said:

> I truly believe that potential is widely distributed but the opportunity is not. I am personally on a journey to create pathways to leadership for diverse founders and investors in tech.
>
> There were two pivotal moments in my career that influenced me to dedicate my career to moving the needle on this problem. The first was when I first started working in the City and would turn up to the office and be 60 per cent of my true self because I didn't feel at home and saw no one in leadership that I could relate to or who even looked like me. I remember feeling like no one understands me or takes an active interest in who I am and where I am from.
>
> The second was an opportunity I had in 2015 to live and work in San Francisco with an organization to kickstart their innovation business, working with leading VCs in Silicon Valley and their startups. That experience validated that I had the skill and aptitude to learn, but the differentiator was that I was afforded the opportunity.

Andy's work has spanned many different startups and organizations, with people coming from all different backgrounds. Less than 10 per cent of all venture capital deals go to women, people of colour and LGBTQ founders. To change this statistic, Backstage Capital has invested over US $7 million in more than 130 companies led by underrepresented founders (Backstage Capital, 2019). I asked Andy, given his extensive experience, what he recommends to new startups to incorporate scaling, equitable environments into their DNA from the beginning. He said:

> Always put people before profits. Treating people fairly in a psychologically safe space where transparency and trust is fostered is crucial for getting the best out people and creating an inclusive environment.

As we go on this journey, incorporating a people-first approach, there will be moments that we can easily think of when we have been able to make a real change and we've felt like this is *why* we do what we do. For Andy, he had a clear example in mind:

> Most recently I was on the Advisory Board of London Tech Week (LTW) where I championed the importance of making tech in London inclusive to all. This meant really working with the Boroughs across London to ensure their voices were heard and acted on when designing an experience for all. We ended up creating Borough Day and working with a range of companies such as The Nest, One Tech, BYP Network, Extend Ventures and others to ensure LTW had great representation across the board.

We will chat about allies more in a few chapters. Given how homogeneous VC funds usually are, there has to be an engagement of people from majority demographics to get this funding for underrepresented founders. The people in a high percentage of positions to fund are from those demographics. I asked Andy how he had engaged allies in any of his roles to push forward meaningful change that didn't solely rely on him or his team. He told me:

> In 2020, after the racial injustices experienced in the United States with George Floyd and the heightened awareness of the Black Lives Matter movement, I was reflecting on what more I can do to support allies within my network.
>
> I then spoke to a colleague who is a white male CEO of a well-known startup coalition bringing together experts. He has been a

helpful ally to me over the years about what more he could do in his position of influence. He went on to release this heartful blog post discussing how disadvantaged Black and BAME founders can be and announced that the company would grant £50,000 to a Black-led angel syndicate group. It was an honour to be on the judging panel for this opportunity. They also launched a programme to support diverse founders through Covid-19.

This is a great example of an ally spending time to understand their privilege, delivering into what is happening in the world and making an actionable difference – in this case, putting his network and money where his sentiments and words were.

Privilege is a topic we all must engage with. I describe myself as underrepresented yet privileged – a woman of colour from a poorer background, but now with financial stability, a Western name/accent who has been adopted into the Western world.

I asked Andy how he, a Black man, had explored his own personal privilege whilst being underrepresented simultaneously:

Perspective is powerful. I remember as a kid feeling that I suffered from relative poverty, living in an environment with a high unemployment and crime rate. I lived in a flat during my early years where I had people living on top of me, beneath me and beside me and I sometimes literally felt trapped in. Fortunately for me, I travelled over the years to various countries such as Brazil, Ghana and South Africa. It became very apparent to me that poverty was relative.

I came to realize that as a young, working class Black boy growing up in Tottenham, I had high potential as well as high access to opportunity, just because I was born in London. However, so many of the young people I met travelling had the same high potential but such low access to opportunity by no fault of their own.

I didn't choose to be born a man, be Black or born in London. I inherited this all from birth. However, as I grow in influence, wealth and privilege, I believe I have a responsibility to use my privilege to address inequalities I am aware of, regardless of whether they affect me or not. From sexism to anti-Semitism.

My advice to people going on this journey now is to always consider the question, 'who is not in the room?' Continuously consider whose voice is not being represented in this meeting, whose perspective is not being considered with the making of this product and whose influence is not being heard at the table of leadership.

From going on this continuous journey, we are creating a personal cycle of self-awareness that allows us to understand how we can do more for those who need it.

References

Accent Bias Britain (2019) [accessed 13 December 2020] Results: Labels [Online] https://accentbiasbritain.org/results-labels/ (archived at https://perma.cc/87L9-C3TA)

Andersson, S (2014) [accessed 13 December 2020] Privilege Walk: A Path Towards Understanding Norms and Stereotypes, DIVA [Online] www.diva-portal.org/smash/record.jsf?pid=diva2%3A854327&dswid=3883 (archived at https://perma.cc/YCH3-UF38)

Backstage Capital (2019) [accessed 13 December 2020] Current Investment Statistics [Online] https://backstagecapital.com/ (archived at https://perma.cc/NX4Q-Z67Y)

Harvard Business Review (2019) [accessed 13 December 2020] Research: Women Score Higher Than Men in Most Leadership Skills [Online] https://hbr.org/2019/06/research-women-score-higher-than-men-in-most-leadership-skills (archived at https://perma.cc/PHM8-LU48)

Heller, J (2020) [accessed 13 December 2020] I'm a Black Startup Founder: Here's How I Raised $11 million After 150 Rejections, *Fast Company* [Online] www.fastcompany.com/90537023/im-a-black-startup-founder-heres-how-i-raised-11-million-after-150-rejections (archived at https://perma.cc/AF65-ELN7)

Huang, L (2020) [accessed 13 December 2020] How to Overturn
Workplace Prejudice about 'Foreign' Accents, www.ft.com [Online]
www.ft.com/content/27ff66f4-35ed-11ea-a6d3-9a26f8c3cba4
(archived at https://perma.cc/9NZV-MG8L)

Human Rights Campaign (2018) [accessed 13 December 2020] Violence
Against the Transgender Community in 2018 [Online] www.hrc.org/
resources/violence-against-the-transgender-community-in-2018
(archived at https://perma.cc/GNB4-LATD)

Leonhardt, D (2013) [accessed 13 December 2020] In Climbing Income
Ladder, Location Matters, *The New York Times*, 22 July [Online]
www.nytimes.com/2013/07/22/business/in-climbing-income-ladder-
location-matters.html (archived at https://perma.cc/J8UD-QPCF)

Menin, A and Ashworth, L (2017) [accessed 13 December 2020]
Cambridge Accepts More Black Men than Etonians for the First Time
on Record [Online] www.varsity.co.uk/news/13366 (archived at
https://perma.cc/3AEL-K9J6)

Mervosh, S and Bogel-Burroughs, N (2019) [accessed 13 December 2020]
Amber Guyger's Judge Gave Her a Bible and a Hug: Did That Cross a
Line? *New York Times*, 4 October [Online] www.nytimes.com/2019/
10/04/us/amber-guyger-judge-tammy-kemp-hug.html (archived at
https://perma.cc/ASK5-WSAL)

Moyers, B (2013) [accessed 13 December 2020] Where You Grow Up
Matters [Online] https://billmoyers.com/2013/07/23/where-you-grow-
up-matters/ (archived at https://perma.cc/YD7R-Z55S)

Oxfam (2019) [accessed 13 December 2020] 5 Shocking Facts about
Extreme Global Inequality and How to Even it Up [Online] www.
oxfam.org/en/5-shocking-facts-about-extreme-global-inequality-and-
how-even-it (archived at https://perma.cc/8S44-83XM)

Womens Aid (2019) [accessed 13 December 2020] Domestic Abuse is a
Gendered Crime [Online] www.womensaid.org.uk/information-
support/what-is-domestic-abuse/domestic-abuse-is-a-gendered-crime/
(archived at https://perma.cc/N3KH-NSNX)

CHAPTER FOUR

Intersectionality

Peeling the onion of differences

This chapter will focus on:

- What is intersectionality and what are its origins?
- How does it work in practice?
- How do we need to recognize this in our daily lives at work?
- Intersectionality on a more personal level

What is intersectionality and what are its origins?

Intersectionality is the overlapping and connected nature of personal characteristics, such as ethnicity, race, socio-economic background, etc. This connected nature creates an overlapped and connected experience of discrimination.

For example, a Black woman might face discrimination from a business that is not distinctly due to her race (because the business does not discriminate against Black men) nor distinctly due to her gender (because the business does not discriminate against white women), but due to a unique combination of the two factors.

This term was created and coined by Kimberlé Williams Crenshaw in 1989, a Black feminist US lawyer, civil rights advocate, philosopher and a leading scholar of critical race theory. Her work has defined, shaped and amplified the need for an understanding of the nuance and intricacies of privilege, discrimination and how society treats people based on these different characteristics.

Before delving into intersectionality, let's talk about critical race theory first. Critical race theory is the view that legal systems and institutions have ingrained and deep-rooted racism, by default, and that race itself is a socially constructed ideology or concept, used by white people to further their own interests and gain power over and at the expense of people of colour.

The past cannot be readily disconnected from the present and future – it all flows together. Critical race theory has been used to examine how institutional racism manifests in instances like housing segregation, bank lending, discriminatory labour practices and access to education. It has also evolved the language and initiatives focused on addressing racism, white privilege, intersectionality and more. It asks us to recognize the historic inequalities that have been deliberately baked into our societies, so we can actively challenge, change and demolish them. This must be done with an intersectional lens.

Originally, the term intersectionality was created because, largely, ethnicity was ignored by first-wave feminism, which broadly focused on the equality between white men and white women. Because of this, many of the early women's rights movements were focused on the struggles of white women, which loses the fight for real inclusion – white women are inherently privileged due to being white. This also highlights how 'whiteness' is viewed as the default or base state.

Second-wave feminism was broadly focusing on the dismantlement of the domestic purpose of women and their existence. Think about gender stereotypes, unequal pay and the restricting of education for those based on gender. This wave achieved success in various ways – mostly through the Equal Pay Act of 1963 and the Title IX federal civil rights law in the United States that was passed as part of the Education Amendments of 1972, which stated that 'No person in the United States shall, on the basis of sex, be excluded from participation in, be denied the benefits of, or be subjected to discrimination under any education program or activity receiving Federal financial assistance'(US Dept of Health and Human Services, 2019). But yet again, women of colour and specifically Black women were largely forgotten about given the extra discrimination these groups of people faced.

When third-wave feminism emerged in the late 1980s, it actively recognized and noted the lack of focus and attention to economic background, sexual orientation, ethnicity and gender identity that the previous movements had. This highlighted that white women (due to white privilege) and men of colour (due to privilege of being a man) held power to both be oppressors whilst still being able to be oppressed.

The creation of the fourth wave and intersectional feminism that continues this work on a deeper level and actively pushes against the focus on white, cisgendered, middle-class women, broadening out focus and ensuring nuance, is included in under-standing how we support those who need it and dismantle systems that may benefit white women but do not benefit other types of women. However, in theory and in practice are two different things.

How does intersectionality work in practice?

We've just completed a Privilege Walk exercise. During this exer-cise, each question is asked to create a wider understanding of how each of our lives has been shaped by things both within and outside of our control and how these limit or create opportunities.

I shared my story at the beginning and there are some elements that, for me, greatly affect how privileged yet disadvantaged

I am. An example is that whilst I am a woman of colour, I have the privilege of having an Irish accent and a Western name, meaning the effect of my ethnicity on how I am treated is decidedly different from those who have non-Western accents/names. My name, for example, will not flag bias during a CV review as it does not highlight that I may be a person of colour with a different ethnicity. However, I am still treated and viewed differently from Irish women with the expected white skin. Again, whilst I am financially privileged now, I did not grow up this way, which meant different barriers to progression for me – from taking out extensive loans and applying for grants to attend university, to not having the privilege of generational wealth to fall back on. I am unable to be viewed by society as singularly a woman, a person of colour, a person from a poorer economic background – society views me as a culmination of these. For me, this also works with the privilege that I have as a cis-gendered, non-disabled, heterosexual woman too. All of these elements work in tandem and in sync with each other – they are not viewed holistically.

As we look at a bias-shaped society, we can see how the focus of those at these intersections and overlaps have been forgotten or actively pushed against. The creation of the term 'white feminism' used today highlights the awareness of this type of feminism that only considers white women worthy of fighting for. It is a privileged view of oppression that many do not have access to.

'White feminism' focuses heavily and is broadly aligned to the first-wave feminism view – homing in on white women equality and disregarding the need for a more nuanced view due to lack of personal engagement or care. There is an assumption that racism, homophobia, classism or ableism is always aggressive, obvious and in your face, when in fact it can be incredibly 'subtle' but deadly.

You might be aware of the Suffragettes, but are you aware of how they disregarded and set Black women to the back of their marches, with Susan B. Anthony exclaiming, 'I will cut off this right arm of mine before I will ask for the ballot for the Negro and not for the woman', entirely disregarding Black women in this fight.

During this time, Sojourner Truth, who had experienced her own fight towards freedom from slavery, commented on this very issue in 1867, when female suffrage was still being discussed:

> I feel that I have the right to have just as much as a man. There is a great stir about coloured men getting their rights, but not a word about the coloured women; and if coloured men get their rights, and coloured women not theirs, the coloured men will be masters over the women, and it will be just as bad as it was before. (Dionne, 2017)

What's also important to note is that people remember the noteworthy line from Truth's speech stating 'Ain't I a woman?' in relation to her experiences as a Black woman. However, we must remember that Truth's first language was Dutch; she didn't learn English until she was older. She was also from New York so it is highly unlikely (quite literally almost impossible) that she had a southern accent or dialect. The original speech was documented by Marius Robinson (who was good friends with Truth); however, in 1863, a white woman named Frances Gage rewrote the speech 12 years later, adding the southern dialect that almost certainly didn't exist (The Sojourner Truth Project, 2014). This is a prime example of how some white women have forced Black women into boxes, enforcing stereotypes and viewing them as one-dimensional. The view that Black women must only have southern dialects and speak like this is racist tropes at best.

When we applaud women like Susan B. Anthony without recognizing the very real and direct damage they have done to women of colour (and specifically Black women), then we cannot say we care about equity or equality – we simply only then care about those we directly identify with. And that isn't good enough.

It's important to remember that white feminism isn't just the focus on 'whiteness' but on the privilege of being heterosexual and middle-class. You also do not have to be white to perpetuate 'white feminism'. Many people of colour also create a positive view towards those who have closer associations to whiteness, as the media, cultures and society have ingrained this into mindsets. This is called colourism and we'll talk about this in more depth in a little bit.

There are lots of subtle ways white feminism ideology can manifest itself:

- The tone policing of people of colour when speaking about racism or their experiences with racism, where it is more offensive to be called a racist than to discuss the actual racism itself.
- When women who embody white feminism are called out on behaviour that actively has hurt or damaged other people, the trope of 'white women tears' being used to re-centre themselves as the victim has actively silenced women of colour into avoiding raising issues that may then see them painted as the aggressor.
- When we view progress towards an equal society being close when, realistically, those who have greatly benefited from diversity and inclusion-related strategies are non-disabled, cis-gendered, economically stable, heterosexual white women. It's important to note that this is because white women are the closest group to white men – therefore benefiting from both this close proximity and also from their whiteness, which is viewed as the default.
- Who we vote for and why. To separate politics and life is a privilege. Depending on who we vote for, poorer people, those in essential working roles, ethnic minorities and more may be detrimentally affected. It's important we think of the impact of our actions outside of those whom we directly identify with. Intention and impact are two very different things and when

we centre our own personal needs only and not those of wider underrepresented or forgotten groups, we lose our power to do things better. An example of this is the treatment of National Health Service workers in the UK during Covid-19, where those who had visas were extended for one year, with no view of what would happen after the year. After saving many lives and keeping the country alive, there is still no security for these people. Or the Windrush scandal, where in 2018, people (particularly from Caribbean countries) who came to the UK and helped build this country, were wrongly detained, denied legal rights, threatened with deportation and, in at least 83 cases, were wrongly deported from the UK by the Home Office (Joint Council for the Welfare of Immigrants, 2020). Or in Northern Ireland that it took until 2020 for gay marriage to be made legal. All of these decisions are made by those in government and perhaps these issues do not affect the majority of the population, but they do affect our people. And separating how we vote with our views/how we show we care is peak white feminism.

When we dive into the impact of a lack of understanding of intersectionality in society we can see clear trends. We've talked about the Suffragette movement and it's lack of inclusivity – due to this, it wasn't until 6 August 1965 that President Lyndon Johnson signed the Voting Rights Act, which outlawed the discriminatory voting practices that many Southern states adopted after the Civil War to restrict Black men and women from voting. Prioritization of any women who were not white was not present in the Suffragette's movement and whilst we may applaud them for some efforts, we must be critical of the racism and direct damage they caused to women of colour.

Before moving on, let's remember that racism isn't always as violent or bold as restricting voter rights. Many people think that just because they don't say the n-word that they aren't racist. Or because they 'treat everyone the same', they're not racist. To be clear, being nice isn't the same as being anti-racist. In the 2020 US Presidential election, despite the overwhelming push for racial equality that very summer, Donald Trump, the then sitting US President known for his divisive rhetoric, received over 70 million votes (Kommenda *et al*, 2020). Trump has not shied away from embracing racism to his advantage, from actively telling the Proud Boys to 'stand back and stand by' when asked to condemn white supremacy (Smith *et al*, 2020), stating that 'laziness is a trait in Blacks' and his unfathomable comments about Mexico, stating at one of his own rallies that 'they're rapists… some, I assume are good people' (Gass, 2020).

Many who were privileged enough to have disconnected from the clear ingrained racism in this leadership and in society, through many of the ways we've spoken about, were shocked at how many people still voted for Trump, despite his behaviour throughout his four-year term. But the fact is, we saw an increase in the number of white women voting for Trump, shifting from 52 to 55 per cent (Essence, 2020), despite all of this. Now, do these people openly 'class' themselves as racist? Likely not, because whilst some of them will be outwardly racist, many will not and claim to be indifferent to race. My personal view is that if you vote for someone and align with someone who clearly spreads racism, division and hatred, then… well, you're racist, whether you publicly say those things or not. The point is, those people were willing to align with someone for their own apparent gain, whilst throwing brown and Black people to the side, the irony being the wave of performative allyship seen in the wake of George Floyd's death that wasn't replicated in the voting booth.

What you will hear from a lot of people is 'I don't see colour' or a proclamation of 'colour blindness' when challenged. It may shock you to know that this is racist, but it is. By not seeing colour, you are making an assumption that all people (regardless of skin colour) are treated the same and, therefore, have all gained access to equal opportunities. That is simply not the case. It is also disregarding the importance of ethnicity and culture to many people. To be anti-racist, we must actively see colour, understand why and how society treats people differently based on it, then move forward with education and awareness. Intersectionality plays an important role when we respond to world events.

In the period immediately after 9/11 researchers noted low birth weights and other poor birth outcomes amongst Arab-named women (which was not prevalent for women with Western/expected US names), a result linked to increased racial and religious discrimination (Lauderdale, 2006).

An area of intersectionality I want us to delve into is colourism and how it works in practice in exclusion and inclusion. This is important given Dr Crenshaw's original mission was to shine a light on the exclusion Black women specifically face. Colourism is the difference in treatment between those who are lighter or darker of the same ethnicity and is formed due to a societal preference to whiteness and Caucasian features. Colourism is a complicated discussion because of how it divides those in terms of opportunities, oppression and 'worthiness' whilst still identifying these groups of people by the same ethnicity.

One part of privilege that I have is that whilst I am a woman of colour, I am still lighter-skinned than darker women of colour – and substantially so. I noticed the difference in treatment for me personally as my brother and I both faced intense racism growing up, being called the n-word, darkies or monkey and more. However, as I moved into adulthood, a lot of the openly aggressive racism stopped and was replaced with sexism. I wasn't getting racial slurs shouted at me on the street now, whereas my brother still was. It's important to note he is significantly darker than I am. There is an immense amount of privilege in how these open actions of racism started to disappear from my life. Many women of colour, namely Black women, don't have things quite so lucky.

Colourism isn't only manifested as racial abuse or attacks. It is also manifested in different, more subtle ways. In Asia, there are multi-billion dollar skin-whitening markets, dedicated to providing the means to lighter and 'more beautiful' skin:

> 'Fair and Lovely' is India's largest selling skin lightening cream, with 24bn rupees ($317m; £256m) in annual revenue in 2019. Ever since the 1970s when it first hit the market, millions of tubes are bought every year by teenagers and young women in a country where lighter skin is routinely equated with beauty. (Pandey, 2020)

In 2020, in the wake of the Black Lives Matter protests, Unilever changed their popular skin-lightening cream name from 'Fair and Lovely' to 'Glow and Lovely' (Unilever, 2020). Does changing a name mean much? A lightening cream is a lightening cream regardless of name. With creams like this and the clear preference for lighter skin, society perpetuates the idea that white skin is better, more beautiful and therefore more worthy.

When we delve into this from an intersectionality perspective, we must recognize that dark-skinned people and specifically darker-skinned Black women are treated worse than their lighter counterparts. The term 'misogynoir', coined by Moya Bailey (Anyangwe, 2015), references the sexism and racism that Black women specifically face – and understanding the nuance that darker Black women face. This is grounded in intersectionality. There are examples of this daily. Think about how the creator of the #MeToo movement, Tarana Burke – a Black woman activist – was forgotten so readily in the stories as Alyssa Milano was lauded for its creation, despite it having existed years prior through Tarana's work. Or the wave of famous lighter-skinned Black 'influencers' who had previous anti-Black tweets brought up in their history actively disparaging, attacking and insulting darker-skinned Black women.

Colourism isn't limited to who finds you attractive or who will marry you either. It has a very real effect on society, with dark-skinned Black people literally having longer prison sentences than their lighter counterparts. A study of 12,000 Black women imprisoned in North Carolina between 1995 and 2009 showed that Black women deemed to have a lighter skin tone received more lenient prison sentences and served less time behind bars (Viglione, Hannon and DeFina, 2011).

Colourism and anti-Blackness is also rife in Asian communities. An example of this that came out on Netflix in the summer of 2020 was *Indian Matchmaking*, a show where a marriage consultant travels globally to meet with families and clients to find out what they want from a partner and find them a match for an arranged marriage.

The premise isn't complicated – children and their families come together, decide what they want from marriage and the matchmaker tries to find it (sometimes successfully but mostly not). What the show has shone a light on is the ever-present caste system in Indian and Asian communities. The subject of skin colour and its direct link to social stature in Indian culture is complicated. People with darker skin are viewed as lesser, ugly and are faced with prejudice within their own community. On the other hand, fairer skinned Indian people are seen as the pinnacle of beauty, intelligence and money. Throughout the show, when asked about their 'marriage criteria', more often than not candidates replied 'fair', with no hesitation from anyone involved (Aravind, 2020). It is clear as well that all of the candidates that are lighter skinned are viewed more favourably by the matchmaker and their potential marriage partners, with one woman, who looks distinctly like another candidate but is darker skinned, being called ugly and being told it will be harder to find her a partner who will accept her.

According to Amnesty International, one in five women have suffered from online abuse in the UK and that Black female MPs are also 84 per cent more likely to experience online abuse in comparison to white women (Amnesty International, 2020). When we delve into the abuse Black women face online, studies have shown:

- Black women were disproportionately targeted, being 84% more likely than white women to be mentioned in abusive or problematic tweets. One in ten tweets mentioning Black women was abusive or problematic, compared to one in fifteen for white women;
- 7.1% of tweets sent to the women in the study were problematic or abusive. This amounts to 1.1 million tweets;
- Black and minority ethnic women were 34% more likely to be mentioned in abusive or problematic tweets than white women. (Amnesty International, 2020)

If we think about how the actual tone of your skin, even if you are from the same ethnicity, affects how society treats people, we should be able to understand how much other differences such as disability, sexual orientation, age, economic background plays into the need for an intersectional approach.

As a personal example, and one of the reasons I decided to branch Women Who Code across the UK was because there was no price-point for women to be involved or attend. If we were to charge even £5 or US $10, would we be excluding women from a lower economic background? Absolutely. If we are to truly reach women of all backgrounds, we must think of how we support and provide opportunities for different groups of people.

We talked earlier about the higher cost of being disabled – let's think about how that intersects with those from a poorer economic background. According to Disability Rights UK, nearly half of everyone in poverty is either a disabled person or lives with a disabled person. There is a much higher likelihood of being in poverty if an adult in the household is disabled, and again, an even higher likelihood if there is a child who is also disabled – under these conditions, the poverty rate is 40 per cent, which is more than twice the rate where there is no disability (Disability Rights UK, 2020). When we consider the higher rate of living for those who are disabled, consider what that means if you are already from a poorer economic background.

How do we need to recognize this in our daily lives in work?

Let's dive into how this kind of exclusive inclusion has affected the workplace. We have seen many organizations proudly champion and talk about their diversity and inclusion work, usually focusing on gender. This might sound fine but let's discuss why it isn't. A Google Article search on 20 August 2020 for 'gender diversity in the workplace' returned about 1,140,000 results, a search for 'ethnic diversity in the workplace' returned about 403,000 results and a search for 'intersectionality in the workplace' returned about 32,000 results. Gender diversity has been in almost every company's board meetings in the 2010s because of mandatory gender pay gap reporting and the historic understanding of women's rights in relation to voting and body autonomy from society in general. What this hasn't considered is that women are not a monolith and existing under all of the same constraints – what are glass ceilings for some are cement roofs for others.

Many organizations will proudly share that they have one or two women in C-suite/Board or executive positions, but upon further investigation they are all heterosexual, white, able-bodied women. In 2020, Fortune 500 rankings include 37 female CEOs, which is progress from 24 in 2018 and 33 in 2019 (Hickey, 2020). In 2019, California became the first state to set a minimum requirement for female board members at publicly held companies.

But let's not celebrate just yet as only three in the Global 500 are women of colour. None of them are Black or Latina. This is an effect of exclusive inclusion and is not good enough.

People have largely accepted that this level of diversity is a win and 'enough'. It isn't. White/Asian women are primarily easier and more comfortable for white/Asian men to hire due to affinity bias (more on this later) and a high likelihood of being surrounded by white women either in their personal lives or workplaces. When we rest our laurels on this exclusive inclusion we are perpetuating a lack of fairly distributed opportunities. If you didn't already know, what was your reaction to the statistic that there are no Black or Latina women in the Fortune 500 CEOs, whilst the number of women from other ethnicities (namely white and Asian) is progressing. It's easy to talk about almost being a gender parity in your organization, but what is your data from an intersectional lens really telling you?

If it shows you the above, now it's time to discuss the cause. What does your promotion data tell you about the progression of women from different ethnicities? What about women of different sexual orientations? What about transgender women? What about poor women? What about women who are a combination of all of these things and more? Another important element to analyse is your retention data and statistics. Perhaps you have a high retention rate paired with a low attrition rate in your business. Have you analysed this from a gender lens, paired with an ethnicity etc lens? Keep in mind that white women (due to their skin colour) and men of colour (due to their gender) both possess the ability to be oppressed and to be the oppressor. Your strategy and reporting must have intersectionality baked into it. A good example of this is how companies primarily report on their gender pay gap and (if they do it) their ethnicity pay gap separately. This means that there is likely more pay inequities for women of colour undiscovered (and therefore unactioned) in your reporting. Ideally, I would love it if organizations did both a gender pay, ethnicity pay and a combination report sharing transparently where they are and where they're trying to go.

Knowing how it *feels* to be a member of more than one underrepresented group in your organization is imperative. If you look at your attrition or retention data only from one lens, you miss the opportunity to capture a potentially growing issue and address it. A study by Catalyst delves into the emotional tax for people of colour in the workplace. They describe this emotional tax as:

> [f]eeling a need to protect yourself from unfair treatment and negative attention inside and outside the workplace [where] you devote time and energy consciously preparing to face each day, which you know comes with the potential for large and small acts of bias, exclusion, or discrimination. (Travis and Thorpe-Moscon, 2019)

The study found that 58 per cent of women and men of different races and ethnicities reported being 'highly on guard' with Black women (58 per cent) and Black men (64 per cent) reporting the highest on this issue (Travis and Thorpe-Moscon, 2019). Their reasons for being highly on guard varied depending on the group:

- Over 40% of Asian, Black, Latinx, and multiracial respondents report being on guard because they anticipate racial/ethnic bias.
- Women (40%) were significantly more likely than men (26%) to report being on guard in anticipation of gender bias.
- Women of colour (24%) are more likely than men of colour (11%) to be on guard because they expect both gender and racial bias.
- Between 13% and 27% of respondents report being on guard because they anticipate bias based on other aspects of their identity, such as physical appearance, physical ability, age, and religious beliefs. (Travis and Thorpe-Moscon, 2019)

This research shows us the very real impact of identifying with multiple marginalized groups within your workplace and how it influences people's behaviours when they come to work.

We will talk about stereotyping bias in more detail later, but it is clear how stereotyping has played into many of these worries. For example, Black people can be viewed as aggressive when being confident, therefore meaning these people spend more time analysing everything they do and say to avoid being viewed in this light. Asian people are hit with the stereotype of being passive and non-dominant, which causes issues when Asian people break this stereotype and are viewed negatively because it isn't 'what's expected of them'. In the research, people referenced issues such as Black women changing their hair for the workplace, transgender people in the media being mocked without colleagues realizing the person beside them identified as trans, and men (in particular men of colour) worrying about being constantly viewed and rated against masculine tropes.

So, what can you do to work to create an environment that lessens and hopefully removes this tax for people of colour, those of different genders, different sexualities, disabilities, neurodiversities and so on?

Listen

You don't know what you don't know. Spend the time with these groups of people listening to their experiences. Make no assumptions and ensure you do not allow any bias to run into what you think they feel. Do this repeatedly and provide a means for this to happen in a way that scales – doing a one-off one-to-one session is not enough.

Action

There is no use to listening if you won't provide action afterwards – otherwise this emotional tax increases and people feel lost. After you've listened, spend time understanding how these experiences are heightened or impacted by your processes. This will involve sharing this information with wider stakeholders such as your C-suite, backing up these experiences with analysis on the retention/attrition of these groups. Be realistic and honest about what you can change within specified time frames. Saying you'll fix everything within one quarter is unrealistic and will just create disappointment.

Rework

This is a continuous journey. What people feel like now may not be how they feel in six months. This is why you must be open to reworking what you do, even if that means rolling back things you thought would be successful. To make reworking easier, invest in an appropriate and robust employee engagement platform that allows you to capture these temperature checks regularly across marginalized groups.

To effect real change we must be willing to be honest and open, not just of our successes but of our shortcomings and of the ways we have perpetuated the issues we are now trying to fix.

Intersectionality on a more personal level...

Think about your family... what does it look like to you? Do you have caring responsibilities for them, either financially, emotionally, physically or all of the above? Is it similar to that of your colleagues or friends? Many of us will have had unexpected caring responsibilities due to Covid-19 and there has been a substantial shift of what expendable income actually means now. For me personally, during the pandemic (where I am already the main earner in my house) I was also supporting my brother and Dad financially, meaning my expendable income was substantially different. If we think about our lives and other people's lives from a household perspective, it is clear that our lives are not shaped only by our personal circumstances but also those of our families. Let's talk about expendable income. Expendable income is the money you have left over after tax, paying your usual bills and the money you spend on 'life admin'.

From a cultural perspective, especially in some Asian and Black communities, there is a given expectation that those earning a salary in the household support other family members. This is important when we consider, for example, the view that young people have more expendable income than older people with children. Wrong.

Trust for London also found that in their 2020 London Poverty Profile '74% of adults in poverty in London (1,050,000) are in working families, up from 62% a decade ago' (Trust for London, 2020). We can't forget that having a regular expendable income is an element of privilege in itself – it provides security and stability.

Religion is also an important point here too, which usually overlaps with ethnicity. The media influences our biases and our responses to world events. Above we talked about the treatment of birthing Arab-named women and low birth weights in response to 9/11. Think about the knock-on effects of the rhetoric around Muslims, immigrants and more from tabloids. Think about how that affects everyday people, therefore affecting their places of work and therefore affecting who else is hired into those places. In 2012/13, 44 per cent of those who identify as Muslim were paid below the National Living Wage and the Joseph Rowntree Foundation found significant differences in risk of poverty based on religion, with a 50 per cent poverty risk for Muslims compared to 18 per cent for the population as a whole (Trust for London, 2014). It is expected for real-world events to have a knock-on effect on society and people. However, this knock-on effect appears to be biased towards non-white, non-Western people. A good example of this is the rise of white domestic terrorists in the United States. Over 50 per cent of mass shootings in the United States between 1982 and February 2020 were committed by white people; however, we do not see this same bias reflected against white people (Statista, 2020a). We also don't see the same biases reflected against men, despite men committing 113 out of 118 of mass shootings (Statista, 2020b). Let's think about why that might be.

The media plays an important role in society's biases. In this example specifically, there is a notable difference in how white terrorists are described vs Black or brown terrorists – even down to who is given the label 'terrorist'. A study by Just Security (Kearns, 2019) showed that Muslim-perpetrated attacks were given, on average, 4.5 times more coverage than attacks by non-Muslims. This study examined media coverage of the 136 terrorist attacks in the United States, as cited in the Global Terrorism Database, between 2006 and 2015:

> Of 146 network and cable news programs between 2008 and 2012 they found that 81% of terrorism suspects that were subjects of news reporting were Muslim, far greater than the percentage of terrorist attacks in the US that were committed by Muslims during the same time period. While some of these suspects may have been outside of the US, there still appears to be over-coverage of Muslims as terrorists. When we consider television news, the trend is the same: Muslims are over-represented as terrorists. (Kearns, 2019)

This behaviour then directly has a knock-on effect on opportunities for those from these communities. Remember, talent is everywhere, but opportunity is not.

I sat down with globally renowned Chief Technology Officer, Chair of the Global Tech Leadership conference series *The Lead Developer*, sitting Treasurer on the Board of Stonewall (an organization which campaigns for the equality of lesbian, gay, bi and trans people across Britain) and self-confessed 'geek manager', Meri Williams, to ask her about how she sees DE&I playing a role in creating the solutions of tomorrow, and how intersectionality is crucial in this discussion.

Before kicking off, I asked Meri why she is so passionate about DE&I efforts and why she actively advocates for this work, every day and in every role she holds:

> As a business leader I support inclusion because it's frankly great business sense. Diverse teams that harness the value of difference have proven again and again to be more innovative, deliver more consistent and better results, and have better

ability to attract, recruit, retain and grow talent. There's also strong evidence that having women and people of colour on an organization's board leads to greater profitability.

I think one thing that people misunderstand though is presuming that all that is needed is diversity. I think diverse teams outperform homogeneous teams because it creates frictions and pauses on decision making before deciding on how to move forward. The healthy team dynamics and practices needed to get people with different backgrounds, experiences and perspectives to agree on the best way forward also promote success. So just adding more diversity doesn't work unless you also do the work to make things inclusive and equitable.

It's also deeply personal to me, as someone who is in an under-indexed group in many ways. I joke sometimes that 'I'm the one the *Daily Mail* warned you about' as I'm a woman working in tech, an immigrant with a job (I 'think' this is worse than being an unemployed immigrant but I have to check the headlines regularly to be sure), someone who is disabled, queer, neurodiverse and godless. And my wife is British, so I can quite easily be accused of 'stealing their women AND their jobs'.

But I grew up white in Apartheid South Africa, where I experienced pretty much the definition of unearned and undeserved privilege. In some ways this has helped me bridge between people accustomed to privilege, as to them sometimes equality can feel like oppression.

Meri has worked in many different organizations that include Healx, Monzo, Procter & Gamble, Government Digital Service, M&S Digital and MOO. What is clear is how different these organizations' sizes are, which does mean a different approach to DE&I. She agrees:

I think that organizational size and maturity do tend to affect the approach taken to DE&I. Whenever I'm involved in smaller or newer organizations it feels like such a gift to be able to bake things in from relatively early on. One doesn't have to accept all the systems and processes and principles being defined and run in biased ways for years or decades before being able to change them.

It also makes me indescribably sad when organizations think they are 'too small' to focus on DE&I. Just as in software it's much cheaper to make changes the earlier you define them in the software development lifecycle, it's much MUCH easier and better to bake DE&I in from early on, and much more expensive to do things in a biased way and then have to refactor and redo everything later.

Meri has been doing this work for years and it's clear it's not always been easy. Her insights are invaluable and I asked her what her main achievements were in the DE&I space – the things she still looks back on and thinks 'YES! That really made a difference'. She said:

In terms of specific wins I've seen:

- P&G was one of the first companies I know of to reassess ALL their HR policies with inclusion in mind. Certainly in Western Europe this was led by a collection of employee affinity groups (including the LGBT network, the People of Colour network, amongst others), but ably supported by the HR function. They had also done a great deal to ensure that interviewing was focused on competencies and past experience, not on potential (because the latter is both hard to predict and immensely biased to who the current types of people are who succeed). I also know in my 10 years there I had a great many more women role models in leadership than many of my peers.
- At GDS, we adapted the (already good) Civil Service interviewing approach to make it even more even-handed. Removing degree requirements where they weren't really necessary, for instance, we did earlier than many other organizations.

- Healx has pioneered the inclusion of Patient Groups in their work, but also employing parents of folks with rare diseases (and people with rare diseases, like myself), with associated work practices allowing plenty of flexibility and accommodation of hospital appointments, illness, mental health challenges that often come with difficult physical conditions and so on.

- At Monzo, even before I joined the organization, I was pleased to see mental health placed at the centre of considerations, and one of my proudest moments as an employee was when in response to some anti-trans rhetoric off the back of a DE&I update the bank from its main Twitter account very strongly supported trans rights to self-identification.

There is a great blend of culture, policy and process changes from Meri, which makes it clear how important it is that this work is intertwined into everything we do at work. DE&I work is breaking down the systems that have been in place for decades (or more) and challenging the status quo. I asked Meri if she had faced any specific frictions or difficulties in her career around this:

> There were a huge number of frictions and difficulties! At P&G when we first formed the LGBTQ+ network in Western Europe, the HR manager who was helping us had a really difficult time. After we announced the new network, she literally had a stream of employees – mostly older white men in the sales organization – come to her to verify that 'we're only allowing this so we can identify and get rid of them, right?' I really admired how as an ally she stepped up into those difficult conversations and defended the network existing and ensured that privacy and anonymity were prioritized, given the broader environment at the time. It's easy for folks to forget that it was still legal to fire someone for being queer in 2003... we really haven't had equal employment rights all that long. And realistically, anyone who was at school when Section 28 was still in place (which made it illegal for homosexuality to

even be discussed in a neutral manner, let alone positive, by teachers – and was used as a broad stick to beat folks with, with a major chilling effect) may have had very anti-LGBTQ+ views. So businesses do have to deal with modernizing some of those points of view if the government and school system have espoused them in the first place. GABLE (the LGBTQ+ employee affinity network) did a lot to try to explain how and why this was a workplace issue — our most successful move here was a series of posters showing the world map and the number of countries that still punished homosexuality with death, imprisonment or even in some places physical punishments like whipping or stoning; we also had one explaining that there were still more countries that would put us to death than allow us to get married (this remained the case up until Ireland legalized same-sex marriage).

It's important that we all realize that fighting against DE&I isn't always as public or violent as stoning someone. Whilst there have been substantial changes (in some areas) with human rights, there is still a very clear bias from many against inclusion. This may not be as obvious as voting against human rights, but micro-actions and quieter obstacles and obstructions can cause an equally negative and uninclusive environment for under-represented groups. I asked Meri about this evolution of response in her experience. She said:

Once it became less socially acceptable to object to diversity and inclusion, the objections became quieter and more insidious. The most common, still today, is that it's important, but just can't be prioritized or afforded. 'We'll get to it when the immediate focus on profitability / survival / whatever is done' tends to be the refrain. Or of course the typical 'we care about race, sexual orientation, trans, religion, disability, etc, but if we can't even get women well-represented when they are 51 per cent of the population, we can't move on to those yet'. The single-strand approach to DE&I has probably been the most damaging approach of all. Twenty years ago, they were saying 'let us work on [binary] gender first, then we'll get to the rest'... and I look around and see that *still* being said decades later. It's very disheartening.

I've spoken a lot about LGBTQ+ above as those are some of my most specific pertinent examples, but as in all DE&I work our biggest wins were when we took an intersectional approach. In every organization I've been a part of, I've tried to bridge the gaps between different affinity groups. Fundamentally we are stronger together, and you can influence a lot more (and hear a lot more of the opportunities to influence) if you are advocating for each other's needs and for an intersectional approach rather than working in silos.

As we've chatted about in this chapter, any DE&I efforts without intersectionality are not DE&I efforts at all. I asked Meri how she actively creates hiring and interviewing processes with intersectionality in mind. She said:

When people can't even see the problem they have no chance of combatting it. So helping people be better at spotting bias, recognizing their own privilege and then actively designing things to level the playing field is important.

In terms of the most impactful things I have done and seen to embed awareness and equitability in approaches:

- Training hiring managers and interviewers on unconscious bias is essential. That way they can start to spot it in themselves, in their fellow interviewers and even in debrief.
- When writing a job spec, running them through Kat Matfield's Gender Decoder or a tool like Textio can be helpful to ensure you have a balance of terms that will appeal to all genders (though the original research presumed binary gender, sadly). Cutting requirements / 'must have' to the bare minimum – literally the list that represents what EVERY candidate you will interview absolutely MUST have. Move everything

else into a 'nice to have' / bonus list, because research shows a difference in what proportion of requirements different people need to have to feel comfortable applying. You never see the true top of your recruitment funnel, ie all the people who thought about the role but didn't actually apply.

- Proper debriefs of every candidate interview set are important too. We've spotted countless times when a woman's past experience is being compared to a man's future potential (which is inherently unfair) or when the single person of colour in the shortlist is being compared not to each of the other candidates, but to the best qualities of all the white candidates combined. It's tempting to want to 'save time' by just having people fill in a form and go with the majority vote, but these discussions and conversations are genuinely important and act as a bias rejector and a further training opportunity for interviewers.

Meaningful steps forward make an impact. What gets measured gets done. Moving on from interviewing and hiring, I asked Meri what her views are on privilege, intersectionality awareness and their impact on organizations creating equitable opportunities. She said:

There's a fantastic talk by Anjuan Simmon where he exhorts an approach to both understanding and then lending privilege. It's a talk that many folks in tech have told me has changed their personal approach, and I think it's great to be aware of how you might be able to lend your privilege – whether it be by deferring speaking opportunities in favour of folks that are typically less represented or having a 'diversity rider' (GDS did well here too, by saying no to panels).

I also suggest doing analysis such as:

- Auditing existing policies and benefits with an inclusive lens can lead to great improvements, eg just thinking about the fact some folks might have elders to look after rather than just children can expand how we think about 'caregivers' and associated needs.

- In a few organizations I have used a model I came up with for assessing all kinds of inclusion and prioritizing adjustments, which essentially consists of three questions I believe people are asking themselves either consciously or unconsciously when deciding whether to join / stay / say yes to a promotion / leave an organization:

  - Am I EXPECTED here? (Does it seem that people like me are expected to be here?)
  - Am I RESPECTED here? (Do people seem to view any differences I display as a feature not a bug?)
  - Can I BE MYSELF and BE SUCCESSFUL here? (Are there some people more senior than me that I can relate to? Are there multiple ways to be successful and to progress here?)

  I use the above model in workshops, first having people highlight areas of opportunity from their own perspective, then assigning people an identity to represent that is different from their own, to ask them to empathize and highlight concerns from that point of view. It makes some people just reflect more and others need to actually research the demographic they are asked to represent before they can contribute – both result in positive reflection and action.

- Within an organization, I've found clearly articulated values and culture are very helpful. Not least because it helps you move from 'culture fit' to 'culture add'.

- Calibration sessions, well facilitated, can make a big difference in terms of making sure performance assessments are balanced and bias is spotted and combatted as much as possible. The follow-up is to use calibration info to prioritize development opportunities, projects etc for those who best deserve them, rather than those who ask the loudest.

Leading on from actionable changes you can make, it's important to know how to measure success. What gets measured, gets done and done right. Metrics play an important role in a successful DE&I strategy – not just your demographic data, but your inclusiveness data and the overlay of your demographic data onto your processes. I asked Meri about how she measures and captures this important data. She said:

> Measurement matters. I think quotas are rife with problems, but at least starting to measure demographic information alongside other info (like recruitment stats, employee engagement) at least gives the opportunity to spot challenges that particular groups are experiencing. At one organization I worked at, we found that LGBTQ+ folks were more likely to have experienced bullying at work AND less likely to report it. Similarly, I have been asked to consult for companies at a loss as to why they cannot hire any women into technical roles. At one, as soon as we added some demographic questions, we could see that almost all women and non-binary candidates were screened out by the employees' screening applications. This turned out to be a few cases of unconscious bias HARD at work. Another organization caused a massive issue for themselves because the CTO had a narrative that some folks from underrepresented groups had been hired 'even though they didn't meet the bar, because we are so desperate for some diversity'… this presumption of lack of ability followed them through their entire career at the company.

> Fundamentally, leaders need to internalize that when there are two equally good candidates, the candidate who adds some new perspective to the team IS more valuable. Even though that might be uncomfortable to talk about, we manage to break through discomfort to get better outcomes and higher profits and better brands in all sorts of other arenas – why not this one too?

We'll talk more about middle-management and leaderships' role in the success of DE&I strategies later on, but Meri has already touched on this here, where it's clear that leaders play an integral role in how a company embraces inclusion and diversity. For her:

> Leaders set the tone. Leaders need to know that every time they shirk their responsibility and purposefully ignore uninclusive actions or behaviours, they are silently endorsing all that poor behaviour. Managers tend to have responsibility for others' careers and I think they have an extra duty of care to develop management and coaching techniques that help them be a good manager to a wide range of people, not just those similar to themselves.

> This starts with understanding through unconscious bias training and similar what the likely bias is someone is already experiencing because of their demographic profile, both at work and out in the world. Then looking out for it and addressing it.

> Concrete examples include ensuring people's achievements and expertise are adequately represented, learning to default to coaching to make themselves more scalable as a manager (as with coaching one helps the individual find their best way forward), not giving advice others can't take (eg men and women are reacted to very differently if they say the exact same thing, so advice of 'I'd do/say this' can backfire massively), learning how to be a good sponsor, and spotting bias in feedback received about their report and sometimes choosing to address it with the colleague who gave the feedback rather than just passing the bias along directly for the employee to deal with. Good managers are good filters – and sometimes good bulletproof vests!

> At the most senior levels (board, C-suite roles) there is a responsibility to make DE&I part of the way a company does business – along with delivering results and displaying appropriate governance. 'You get what you measure' as is often quipped, so if you want to see managers and leaders improve,

you need to provide appropriate training / re-education AND then hold people accountable for their results.

What I'd like all of us to do is to be aware of how our biases, prejudices and preferences influence every single decision we make – in business, in our lives, with our families, everything. The main point of all of this chapter is to help us dig into the hard truth that privilege and discrimination are layered and nuanced. There is no separation of being different for reason X or reason Y – both of those reasons create an entirely new reason Z. I am unable to have society treat me only based on me being a woman, or being a person of colour, or being from a poorer economic background, or being heterosexual, or being financially stable now – they all come together and create a collated view.

There is nuance here and when we go through our daily lives, it's important to remember and take stock.

References

Amnesty International (2020) [accessed 13 December 2020] Women Abused on Twitter Every 30 Seconds: New Study [Online] www.amnesty.org.uk/press-releases/women-abused-twitter-every-30-seconds-new-study (archived at https://perma.cc/2LSU-H5R2)

Anyangwe, E (2015) [accessed 13 December 2020] Misogynoir: Where Racism and Sexism Meet, *The Guardian* [Online] www.theguardian.com/lifeandstyle/2015/oct/05/what-is-misogynoir (archived at https://perma.cc/PHE7-8BDJ)

Aravind, N (2020) [accessed 13 December 2020] Netflix Reality Hit Indian Matchmaking Tells Some Dark Truths About Life in My Community, *The Independent*, 23 July [Online] www.independent.co.uk/voices/indian-matchmaking-netflix-reality-tv-india-arranged-marriage-sexism-colourism-a9634021.html (archived at https://perma.cc/2YKU-493Y)

Dionne, E (2017) [accessed 13 December 2020] Women's Suffrage Leaders Left Out Black Women, *Teen Vogue* [Online] www.teenvogue.com/story/womens-suffrage-leaders-left-out-black-women (archived at https://perma.cc/B4F6-W85Q)

Disability Rights UK (2020) [accessed 13 December 2020] Nearly Half of Everyone in Poverty is Either a Disabled Person or Lives with a Disabled Person [Online] www.disabilityrightsuk.org/news/2020/february/nearly-half-everyone-poverty-either-disabled-person-or-lives-disabled-person (archived at https://perma.cc/JCQ2-G2YX)

Essence (2020) [accessed 13 December 2020] 55 Percent Of White Women, 18 Percent Of Black Men Voted For Donald Trump: Exit Poll [Online] www.essence.com/news/politics/55-percent-white-women-trump-election-2020/ (archived at https://perma.cc/X265-M9LV)

Gass, N (2020) [accessed 13 December 2020] 15 Most Offensive Things That Have Come Out of Trump's Mouth [Online] www.politico.eu/article/15-most-offensive-things-trump-campaign-feminism-migration-racism/ (archived at https://perma.cc/VNY7-X9QD)

Hickey, A (2020) [accessed 13 December 2020] Morning Brew [Online] www.morningbrew.com/daily/stories/2020/05/18/fortune-500-rankings-include-37-female-ceos (archived at https://perma.cc/66RK-QTRM)

Joint Council for the Welfare of Immigrants (2020) [accessed 13 December 2020] Windrush Scandal Explained [Online] www.jcwi.org.uk/windrush-scandal-explained (archived at https://perma.cc/R9FC-KNDS)

Kearns, EM (2019) [accessed 13 December 2020] How News Media Talk About Terrorism: What the Evidence Shows, *Just Security* [Online] www.justsecurity.org/63499/how-news-media-talk-about-terrorism-what-the-evidence-shows/ (archived at https://perma.cc/D5LW-X4E8)

Kommenda, N, Voce, A, Leach, A, Hulley-Jones, F and Clarke, S (2020) [accessed 13 December 2020] US Election 2020 Results Live: Biden Wins Presidency, Defeating Trump, *The Guardian* [Online] www.theguardian.com/us-news/ng-interactive/2020/nov/07/us-election-2020-live-results-donald-trump-joe-biden-presidential-votes-pennsylvania-georgia-arizona-nevada (archived at https://perma.cc/5EL7-QYPL)

Lauderdale, DS (2006) Birth outcomes for Arabic-named women in California before and after September 11, *Demography*, **43** (1), pp 185–201

Pandey, G (2020) [accessed 13 December 2020] Fair and Lovely: Can Renaming a Fairness Cream Stop Colourism? *BBC News*, 25 June [Online] www.bbc.co.uk/news/world-asia-india-53182169 (archived at https://perma.cc/NTE2-KBFA)

Smith, D, Beckett, L, Singh, M and Wong, JC (2020) [accessed 13 December 2020] Donald Trump Refuses to Condemn White Supremacists at Presidential Debate, *The Guardian*, 30 September [Online] www.theguardian.com/us-news/2020/sep/29/trump-proud-boys-debate-president-refuses-condemn-white-supremacists (archived at https://perma.cc/T6TC-HPBW)

Statista (2020a) [accessed 13 December 2020] US: Mass Shootings by Race 1982–2020 [Online] www.statista.com/statistics/476456/mass-shootings-in-the-us-by-shooter-s-race/ (archived at https://perma.cc/36ND-ECSB)

Statista (2020b) [accessed 13 December 2020] US: Mass Shootings by Shooters' Gender [Online] www.statista.com/statistics/476445/mass-shootings-in-the-us-by-shooter-s-gender/ (archived at https://perma.cc/E4ZA-X9NT)

The Sojourner Truth Project (2014) [accessed 13 December 2020] Compare the Two Speeches [Online] www.thesojournertruthproject.com/compare-the-speeches (archived at https://perma.cc/ET76-JRXA)

Travis, D and Thorpe-Moscon, J (2019) [accessed 13 December 2020] Day-to-Day Experiences of Emotional Tax Among Women and Men of Color in the Workplace [Online] www.catalyst.org/wp-content/uploads/2019/02/emotionaltax.pdf (archived at https://perma.cc/2DV9-5N25)

Trust for London (2014) [accessed 13 December 2020] Inequalities and Disadvantage in London: Focus on Religion and Belief [Online] www.trustforlondon.org.uk/news/inequalities-and-disadvantage-london-focus-religion-and-belief/ (archived at https://perma.cc/XT3R-GHSW)

Trust for London (2020) [accessed 13 December 2020] London's Poverty Profile 2020 [Online] www.trustforlondon.org.uk/publications/lpp2020/ (archived at https://perma.cc/YV7R-QL6G)

Unilever (2020) [accessed 13 December 2020] Unilever Evolves Skin Care Portfolio to Embrace a More Inclusive Vision of Beauty [Online] www.unilever.com/news/press-releases/2020/unilever-evolves-skin-care-portfolio-to-embrace-a-more-inclusive-vision-of-beauty.html (archived at https://perma.cc/PWJ4-TA36)

US Dept of Health and Human Services (2019) [accessed 13 December 2020] Title IX Education Amendments, HHS.gov [Online] www.hhs.gov/civil-rights/for-individuals/sex-discrimination/title-ix-education-amendments/index.html (archived at https://perma.cc/7VMA-S277)

Viglione, J, Hannon, L and DeFina, R (2011) [accessed 13 December 2020] The impact of light skin on prison time for Black female offenders, *The Social Science Journal*, 48 (1), pp 250–58

CHAPTER FIVE

Check yourself

Unchecked and unconscious biases

This chapter will focus on:

- What is unconscious bias?
- What is unchecked bias?
- How do they differ?
- The impact of these biases on society, workplaces and our daily lives.

If you're reading this book, you'll have likely already heard a little (or a lot) about unconscious bias. I want to start from the very beginning of what this means, the difference between unconscious bias and unchecked bias and the real-world implications of these biases.

What is unconscious bias?

Let's start with unconscious bias. Unconscious actions are actions we do without real thought or realizing their impact – the act of doing something or behaving a certain way without self-realization. When I think of unconscious reactions, I think of this almost like muscle memory, where you don't even have to think about what you're doing, you just do it. Think about it. If you know how to drive, when you get into the car, do you think about how you go through the many steps before even setting off – you put on your seat belt, put the key in the ignition, check your mirrors, release the gear stick, check around the car, put the car into gear, balance the pedals properly and only then do you move forward. But these things all happen without a lot of thought because, realistically, you'll likely have been doing them for quite a while – they are second nature.

Unconscious actions, when not challenged, breed unconscious outcomes. Now, I want us to remember that intention and impact are not the same thing – they do not always align, and a true ally (more on what this is later!) will recognize, learn and adapt when this happens. Unconscious outcomes may not always be negative, but they have the ability to be, and that is enough for us to ensure we challenge ourselves and make sure we're making decisions without bias feeding in.

At the very beginning of this book, I briefly talked about the example of walking home and how, under different lenses, these have different impacts on people – nonchalance, fear, anxiety, to name but a few. The biases we have either for or against people are regularly unconscious and are a product of how we have been raised since children, where we have grown up, who was around us during these formative years, our own personal experiences, who our friends are/were, the media and the lifestyles we and those around us have had. These all piece together to affect how we think and feel about certain types of people.

What is unchecked bias and what's the difference between unconscious and unchecked bias?

Unconscious bias can be rooted in a lack of awareness and blissful ignorance and there is an element of absolving those who perpetuate it because they simply 'don't know better'. I view unchecked bias as the biases that we see around us (either self-perpetuating or in others) and do not challenge, because we don't want to or don't deem the effort of challenging worthy. Unchecked bias means you're aware of these things yet do not wish to rectify or change your behaviour or challenge others.

I remember an instance of this happening vividly in my career. A C-suite member was rolling out a new inclusion initiative focused on supporting disabled people but was using ableist language (that is language that is actively viewed as offensive or exclusionary by disabled communities). When I raised it, I was told that 'we know it's not acceptable, but we have to pick our battles with this person so we'll let them continue to use it'. I pushed again and escalated the issue but wasn't listened to. Back then, I was much more junior. Now, the problem here is that no one in the room directly identified with being disabled and therefore didn't deem this instance worth fighting for. Is that good enough? Absolutely not.

Before we discuss the impact of unconscious and unchecked bias, I want us to remember again that intention and impact do not always match up. If your bias is unconscious or unchecked, realistically the outcomes may be similar to those who are being disadvantaged or hurt because of them. There is the nuance that unchecked bias is worse because it is known to not be acceptable, yet it still happens. However, I would argue that regardless of the type of bias, the hurt is equally as important. Remember that we must not centre the person causing the hurt or disadvantages and their feelings – we must always be open to be wrong, to not centre ourselves if we're perpetuating bias (unconsciously or otherwise) and to learn from these events. Remember, they will happen – to me, to you and to everyone. It's about what we do when they happen that's important. We must take ownership of our biases – and rework them. More on that in the next chapter.

Unconscious and unchecked bias plays a crucial role in why society is still so unbalanced, despite laws and regulations around equality and protected characteristics being commonplace. These internalized automatic knee-jerk reactions cause very real and dangerous inequalities.

What are the main biases we see in work and our daily lives?

There are many biases that are present. Here are some of them and how they work in practice in a workplace.

Affinity bias

Affinity bias is our unconscious (or conscious) likelihood to get along and bond with others who are like us, in one or more ways. By human nature, it's easier to spend time, integrate or socialize with people who are the same as us because it allows for group think, an echo chamber and a lower chance of friction or differing opinions. We are drawn to people like us because we see ourselves and our experiences in them, therefore we feel like we can relate to them.

HOW DOES THIS AFFECT BUSINESSES?
Affinity biases create an easier path to enter, progress and stay in a business for those who are more similar to those who are already there. Think of it this way – if all of your C-suite members are white, straight men and approximately 70 per cent of your middle management are also white, straight men – if you are a white, straight man and join, it is easier for the people interviewing and deciding who is promoted to want you in the organization and want you to stay. There is a direct alignment between you and those people. If you do not identify with one or several of those attributes, the gap to bridge is much bigger.

WHAT CAN WE DO ABOUT IT?

Awareness, analysis and accountability are all key. There must be an awareness of the demographic breakdown of your organization's hiring pipeline and internally, at all levels (not just executive), with this data then being put across promotion rounds to understand who is and isn't being promoted. You cannot know where you are going if you don't know where you're at right now.

This analysis should be run quarterly and, if notable trends are present, transparent conversations and actions, such as mandatory privilege training and the implementation of initiatives such as the Rooney Rule to diversify your pipeline, should be undertaken. The Rooney Rule, originally created by the National Football League in the United States, is a policy that requires league teams to interview ethnic minority candidates for head coaching and senior football operation jobs. There is no hiring quota or hiring preference given to minorities, only an interviewing quota so it widens the pool and forces the NFL into interviewing more diverse groups of candidates before making a decision. Many companies have implemented a version of this where they don't make a decision on who to hire without having interviewed at least two women and/or people of colour at the final stage.

Attribution bias

Attribution bias relates to the systematic errors people make when they're evaluating their own or other people's behaviours. Humans are flawed and our biases are no different. A good example of attribution bias is how we view our successes as our doing and our doing only, whereas we tend to blame failures on external influences or people. Or how if someone drives out in front of you, you are immediately angry and think they are a bad driver or a selfish person rushing; however, if it were you, you may use the excuse that you were rushing to get somewhere important.

HOW DOES THIS AFFECT BUSINESSES?

Studies have found that if something bad happens to someone else, people blame that person's behaviour or personality 65 per cent of the time. But, when something bad happens to them, they blame themselves only 44 per cent of the time, and they blame their situation much more (Ethics Unwrapped, 2013). This affects businesses by ultimately having one rule for one person and another rule for someone else – it breeds inequality and unfairness.

A side effect of having one rule for yourself and a different rule for others is resentment in the workplace. Let's consider the following scenario. If a director or senior leader sees no issue with their constant lateness because they have childcare but then take issue with a middle manager doing the same thing because they expect them to be in the office, that breeds resentment. Resentfulness is not a healthy emotion to have in the workplace.

WHAT CAN WE DO ABOUT IT?

We must be ethical with how we work – and be fair, to both others and ourselves. This is common sense – don't do one thing and say another. 'Do as I say and not as I do' is not a healthy motto for any workforce. What we can do about this is to take a moment when we see ourselves being harsh on people to really evaluate if we're being fair. Ask yourself 'would I have this same reaction if it were me or someone close to me doing this?' and note whether you've been seeking context from the person for the reason of the actions. This takes time to untrain ourselves, so get ready to go on a journey.

Recency bias

Recency bias occurs when we remember people more favourably when we have interacted with them more recently. This bias plays on our memory and how we're able to access those memories more easily and therefore the people attached to them.

HOW DOES THIS AFFECT BUSINESSES?

Recency bias is notable in the workplaces where there are people who go on leave and then return. This may be down to caregiver leave (when people have children, either biologically or otherwise), therefore taking extended periods of time away to spend with a new family member. Or, as we have seen in 2020 during the global pandemic, in the UK, many organizations put employees on furlough, where the government paid 80 per cent of their salaries to help businesses weather the storm. Or, for disabled employees, long periods of leave may be needed for treatment or rest.

This is also present in interview processes, where interviewers can recall the most recently interviewed candidates better than the candidates interviewed earlier.

WHAT CAN WE DO ABOUT IT?

For current employees, there must be a support network and mechanisms in place to support those going on and coming back from longer periods of leave. This should involve having honest one-to-one conversations before they go to understand where they are in their career, if they want contact whilst they are off, and capturing detailed feedback on their current and previous assignments (you should be doing this anyway!). When they come back, set them up with a buddy in the same remit as them to help ease them back into work, have a detailed FAQ with a list to any important company updates they may have missed, signpost mental health resources, be clear that you expect them to need time to settle back in and ensure conversations are had with their manager to provide this support (if you say that you're providing this time to ease them back in and then your employee is punished for not being able to keep up right away, you are being part of the problem).

When it comes to performance reviews or promotion rounds for those who have extended leave in their path, rely on the detailed feedback captured at the time of their leave and their output on assignments. It is easy to disconnect if you don't see someone for several months, but we must do better.

For interview candidates, take detailed notes of every interview, using a template. Find a method that works for you, whether it is bullets, drawings or something else and utilize it to avoid missing important facts and trying to then form a memory later, which can be inaccurate.

Stereotyping

Stereotyping is a common bias that many of us will have either heard of or directly experienced. We hear about stereotypes in the media, in work and in our daily lives. Stereotyping is when we assume something about a person because they belong to a certain group. Our brains try to make decisions faster by making these biased connections or assumptions.

There are lots of damaging stereotypes out there. Are there any that have directly affected you or the people around you? How about the stereotype that women are too emotional or that they won't want that promotion because they have responsibilities like children? Or that 'real men' don't cry or show emotion? The list goes on...

HOW DOES THIS AFFECT BUSINESSES?

Stereotyping can play a big role in who is hired, who progresses and who stays in your organization. This can be impactful especially in hiring departments and interviewers should ensure they do not fall prey to stereotypes and prejudices related to different people.

WHAT CAN WE DO ABOUT IT?

Applicants should be selected purely on the basis of sufficient job-related skills and talents. For example, it is very common to hire more men than women due to personal biases or gender stereotypes. It is also much more common to hire white people than people of colour because of the faces and types of people that we are used to seeing in leadership positions (and because of who is usually doing the hiring). We are also creating a generalization and an understanding that we believe those people may be better at job X simply because more people from those backgrounds are doing those roles at the minute. However, that does not mean that there are people from other groups that are not just as or more qualified and we should really challenge ourselves through the interview process to make sure we are not making assumptions in this way.

Halo/horn bias

Halo/horn bias is primarily found in the hiring and interviewing process. This is where an interviewer allows one strong point about the applicant to overshadow or have a positive or negative on everything that comes afterwards.

If it's a halo, it's something that they've liked, and if it's a horn, it's something that they disliked. Either way, this bias clouds all other responses from the applicant, causing the process to be rife with interference, opinion and bias.

HOW DOES THIS AFFECT BUSINESSES?

There are lots of examples of this affecting who is hired. Here are a few.

Horn bias – an applicant is interviewed and cannot converse well in English. Now, even if their job does not require them to have this skill, the interviewer (who can converse well in English) may view the applicant as less intelligent and let this one issue affect their entire interview. The issue here is that this person could have been an excellent fit for the role but could still be rejected purely based on something like this.

Halo bias – an applicant is interviewed and reveals their political views and if it matches with the interviewer, they might prefer that person over others just because of this fact.

The same issue can happen with people in work that we like as opposed to those we dislike. You don't have to be friends with everyone in work but you should be treating people fairly, regardless of whether you personally like them or not.

Similar to affinity bias, the key is the same type of analysis that unearths these unfair processes. We have to be acutely aware of what we're doing and how we're doing it. Your organization should use 360 degree feedback to hear from those in more junior and mid-tier positions who might not be as comfortable raising directly that they've noticed their manager or leader prefers people who are X over people who are Y.

More often than not, you'll hear responses like 'Well, I'm not biased' or 'I always choose the best person for the job' or 'I'd never think someone was lesser because of X'. These are not useful because they allow people to seek refuge in being 'nice' or different from everyone else. Remember that each of these biases does not exist in a vacuum – they overlap and link to each other. We are all biased and there is only one way to change it – accept it and rework our thinking.

The impact of these biases on society, workplaces and our daily lives

Let's go through some examples.

Medical treatment of Black people vs white people

There are various studies showing a clear discrepancy in how Black people are treated, in comparison to their white counter-parts. An example of this is the successful birthrate for Black mothers vs white mothers.

In 2019, in the UK, the chance of death was 1 in 2,500 for Black women (MBRRACE, 2016). However, this rate was five times smaller for white women between 2014 and 2016. In the United States, the rate of pregnancy-related deaths among Black women is three to four times higher than among white women (Kasprzak, 2019). There are a number of things at play here – the intersection of Black women and poorer economic backgrounds, therefore having inadequate access to healthcare, which is especially important in the United States where the average cost of having a child is just over US $10,000 (Hoffower and Borden, 2019), but also the issue that Black women's pain is not listened to in the same way that white women's is. We regularly hear the stereotype of the 'strong Black woman' and the association of strength to women of this ethnicity, which has had a knock-on effect on how serious their claims of pain are taken.

Studies have shown that there are false beliefs such as Black people having literally thicker skin or a higher pain threshold, meaning medical professionals have believed they can suffer or are able to take more pain than their white counterparts (Hoffman *et al*, 2016).

When an assumption is made that person X can withhold greater pain than person Y, purely on their ethnicity and race, we are making a decision to determine that one person is more worthy of being listened to appropriately – whether that is the intention or not, this is the impact.

Lack of women in senior leadership positions

This is one that you've probably heard the most about. Earlier, we talked about the gender bias and stereotypes that have had a knock-on effect on our gender diversity across the board. Let's focus in on senior leadership. Bias plays a huge role on who is deemed 'appropriate' for leadership and ready to be a leader.

We know that there are more people who identify as men in leadership positions in politics, media, technology and more. We are brought up with the majority of people making waves being men. This creates an assumption that men are more capable than women to be leaders. This is rooted in stereotypes. Remember that being the first or one of the first to do something will always come with friction, dismay and doubt because it is unexpected, therefore untested and, at times, feared. Take this issue and overlap it with the societal view of women being the parent to stay at home or to own the main household responsibilities. The bias that tells you a woman won't be the right fit because a role requires travel and she either 1) has children or 2) will want to have children and therefore be unable to do the role, is unconscious and unacceptable. We cannot and should not make assumptions on what people do or do not want.

Differing treatment of people based on ethnicity

Unconscious and unchecked bias against those from different ethnicities has very real effects. The world readily views 'white' as the default, with every other ethnicity as different or as a minority, even in countries where white people are readily the minority. If whiteness is directly viewed as the best, the most intelligent, the worthiest and therefore as supreme, then we have created and allow the continuation of white supremacy to exist. This has absolutely had effects in all parts of our lives.

In the UK, white job applicants were found to be 74 per cent more likely to have success than applicants from ethnic minorities with identical CVs (Sippitt, 2015). These decisions and biases are not limited to our workplaces only. They also affect education and education pathways. University professors were found to be far more likely to respond to emails from students with white-sounding names (Jaschik, 2014). Think about how this creates a barrier to learning, education and growth. How do we expect students with non-white sounding names to progress at the same rate if their growth ultimately has a barrier with their professors? There is an unfair and unjust barrier that cannot be removed without challenging our own dangerous biases.

These biases bleed into every part of our lives. I want you to think personally about how you view white people, Black people and brown people. Be honest with yourself. You have to see colour to truly understand how a bias-shaped society is formed. Think about what ethnicity you are yourself and how you view other people of different ethnicities. Remember that racial prejudice is not limited only to white people. For example, anti-Blackness is rife in Asian communities due to the complex history around colourism and caste systems.

Studies have shown that white participants were found to perceive and view Black faces as more threatening than white faces with the same expression (Jacobs, 2017). Think about what that means... if you view someone as more threatening (for no reason), would you want to work with them? Be friends with them? Hire them? Promote them? What if you are in a position of power or leadership? What if you are in the police and have an ability to stop and search them? In 2020:

> [y]oung Black men were stopped and searched by police more than 20,000 times in London during the coronavirus lockdown – the equivalent of more than a quarter of all Black 15- to 24-year-olds in the capital. More than 80 per cent of the 21,950 searches between March and May resulted in no further action. The figures equate to 30 per cent of all young Black males in London, though some individuals may have been searched more than once. (Grierson, 2020)

Remember that these choices have impacts on real people – they do not happen in an echo chamber.

Bias against disabled people

Firstly, let's remember that not all disabilities are visible. The employment statistics for disabled people paint a very clear picture. In the United States the unemployment rate for disabled people is 6.1 per cent, twice that of people without disabilities (Engler, 2019). The view that disabled people cannot do the things that non-disabled people can do is bias. There may be things that one person cannot do that another can, but this shouldn't be determined on the assumption that, for example, this person uses a wheelchair, has a mental health condition, or has any disability.

It's important to remember how these biases have played into the technology we all use. Research has shown that speech recognition software works less accurately for people with atypical speech patterns, such as those who are deaf (Guo *et al*, 2020). Another concern is the use of AI in processes such as hiring and how having a disability can be viewed as automatically negative by these systems. Google researchers found that machine learning systems were automatically associating a negative 'toxicity' score when sentences mentioned disability (and specifically mental illness) because these had not been appropriately challenged or developed with inclusivity in mind (Hutchinson *et al*, 2020).

If we automatically do not include atypical speech patterns in our solution creation, then we have built in an inherent bias against those using the software. How do we fix this? If we are in a position to influence and call for change, we must test appropriately and rectify these mistakes.

These are just a few examples. I'd like you to think about other biases you've experienced. Can you think of two to five ways you personally treat people differently based on their characteristics or traits – now also think about two to five different ways you may have been treated based on other people's biases towards you...

For your own biases, think about where and how you were raised, your experiences growing up, defining life moments, who you surround yourself with and why. Think about what unconscious decisions you may now make because of those events – who you like and don't like, places you like and don't like to be in, people you want to work with and people you don't, who you assign new opportunities to and who you don't.

For any biases you have experienced, think about decisions that have been made about you irrespective of your input, experience or background. Think about life-shaping or well-known events that have surrounded people similar to you or from a group that you identify with, and think about how they may have caused people to now treat you differently.

Remember how gender, ethnicity, race, religion, disability, neurodiversity, age, sexual orientation, socioeconomic background, caring responsibilities all play into biases. Think about those different steps forwards and backwards in the Privilege Walk and what the reasons are for those steps being forwards and backwards. When people and groups of people are different from the societal default (which is usually white, heterosexual, cisgendered, non-disabled, financially stable men), their existence is more uncomfortable as it is less associated with the groups we are used to seeing regularly in our lives in positions of power and in leadership.

To discuss bias in industry, community engagement and the creation of a scalable global community with inclusion at its core, I sat down with Kike Oniwinde, CEO and Founder of BYP (Black Young Professionals) Network. They empower Black professionals around the world to connect with each other and access opportunities with global corporations. After the 2016 Black Lives Matter protests, the BYP network was founded to harness the power of the Black community. Kike herself is nothing short of phenomenal. Previously a Team Great Britain athlete in Javelin, now a Forbes 30 under 30, she founded BYP Network, and in 2020, raised over US $1.1m on an equity crowdfund – something that only 35 Black women (including herself) have ever done (as of 2018) (Gagné, 2018).

Kike's work is exemplary and BYP has made significant contributions since its creation four years ago. I asked Kike about her driving force for creating the organization that's mission is to 'change the Black narrative', what her goals were back then and if they have changed now four years later. She said:

> No, nothing's changed. And I always think about that. Our mission is consistent – to change the Black narrative. And obviously, we're here now with the uprising of the Black Lives

Matter movement again [I interviewed Kike shortly after the murder of George Floyd, alongside the call for justice for Breonna Taylor and Elijiah McClain and the shooting of Jacob Blake]. It still feels like nothing has changed. There's a huge global problem in the support of Black communities – the police brutality, knife crime rates, how the African continent is depicted globally as poor and corrupt.

Four years ago, I felt very overwhelmed, but also very powerless. I had recently just come back from studying in America and recently started my grad job. But I was on Twitter and I was tweeting, quote tweeting and feeling triggered about the police brutality videos on the timeline. I had to ask myself 'What was the solution to our problems?' I was also thinking about my own attainment and the opportunities I received for me in education and employment. The Black community wasn't represented enough across different organizations and industries. I was seeing how our community was in the most deprived and underfunded areas where knife crime rates were increasing and we were disproportionately overrepresented in prison. There's so many negative statistics and news on our community and I knew this all needed to change – I was fed up.

As someone who was an international athlete with a scholarship to go to the University of Florida and with past experiences of interning in investment banking, I had a lot of opportunities because I was a high achiever, but there was a moment where my eyes really opened. I had gotten a job after I graduated but so many of those who graduated with me couldn't. I realized that being Black in this world was seen as a negative thing and that there were people that hated us for our skin colour.

There was no Black representation on TV outside of sports or music. I realized that we were only ever the entertainment. I became an athlete because it was one of the few things open to me and given how many Black athletes there are and were, becoming an athlete was success for me. The skills you learn from music and sports are invaluable, but there are hundreds of other industries that aren't visible to Black people but also provide incredible skills. To actually become a Usain Bolt or a Beyoncé is one in a billion and many fall by the wayside trying. However, across different industries success is relative and you can still have a great life as an engineer, music agent, project manager etc – attainment that isn't limited for only the best.

I sat down and thought that a great way to change this was to come together as a community. I couldn't be the only one thinking this way, there must be more of us. How do I find other people that are like-minded and want to change the Black narrative? I could only start where I was – by myself, in my room, on my own laptop, with my own energy. So I started with hosting networking events, then growing a mailing list, then launching an app. The idea was always centred on BYP being a global solution. And that hasn't changed. The growth of BYP has only been because it's a big vision and has a real pure intent of changing the world and changing the Black narrative.

So even though we've achieved all of this, we haven't even scratched the surface – we're still dealing with inexperienced and poor DE&I in organizations, we're still protesting, we're still feeling like second-class citizens.

Kike's impact already in four years is impressive. She is impressive. We regularly hear the phrase 'Black excellence', showcasing and empowering Black people being brilliant at their work and doing amazing things. An important discussion that must also be had is how we ensure we as an industry and our organizations support Black people, whether they identify with 'Black excellence' or not. I asked Kike about her thoughts on how we must ensure we support all of these people. She said:

That is something that we talk about at BYP Network regularly. I hate the fact that we have to work 10 times harder or that we have to push excellence to even get a foot in the door. But the reality is, that is the barrier to entry. Take me for example. I've raised US $1.1 million in equity crowdfunding and I am only the 35th Black woman to do that – in the world. That's insane. When it's so normal for people that don't look like me to raise that amount of money. These are things we must break. The sad reality is that the way the world works right now is that the industry requires only excellence from us to even get a foot in the door. And our level of excellence must be substantially more than the white man, who can be mediocre but was handed privilege.

Keep in mind that my crowdfund wasn't venture capital. There are so many barriers that make getting that money super difficult. For us to be able to support the average Black person, we have to break down the system that tells us we must be excellent even to get a foot in as this is just another element of gatekeeping. Corporations are looking for exceptional Black people, just to underestimate, underpay and not promote them. We're still celebrating so many firsts – first Black woman CEO of company X, first Black person in certain political positions and more. And again, these people have had to be extremely excellent. Right now, Black excellence is the only way to push down these doors, but it must change.

We've talked about unchecked and unconscious bias in this chapter. Given Kike is a young Black woman who is very open about the barriers she has had to push against, I asked her if the biases she faces now are the same ones as she faced at the start of her career and if her success had changed this for her. She said:

The barriers persist, right? They've not gone anywhere. This has been a four-year journey right now to get to a place of raising this amount of money and having this platform – it does not take this long for an average white man in this world to get here. Like I said, we still haven't raised VC money. Even now, organizations are speaking about wanting to hire more Black talent and there's an active push, but the barriers in the process still exist with hiring managers still querying if the Black person is good enough, without realizing or educating themselves on their biases, such as being more drawn to white women because they're white too and feeling like they can relate to them more. It's not just up to us to break down these processes and biases – we need allies and we need people to wake up to it.

We'll talk more about allyship in detail later, but Kike has also touched on it here. The Black communities cannot be the only groups interested in supporting, advocating and promoting them. Given the success of BYP, I asked Kike about any allies she has had that have made a meaningful difference and what those specific actions were:

The best allies have been those that have invested in us. The people who work for corporations who say they want to work for us and sign it off with budget. They might not be a Black person – they might be white, Asian or anyone else. Those people who have advocated for us are allies. Our investors are also our allies. We have investors of all different ethnicities, based all over the world. It's important to remember that many investors see the financial opportunities, but they also invest in the person. And there is bias in that process that makes it harder for people like me to succeed. Other allies we have are the people who come to our events, who speak at our events, who speak on our webinars to educate and bring communities together.

Being an ally is very simple – it is just not being racist and opening your eyes to the privilege you have compared to your Black counterparts. I don't need 'colour blind' allies who don't see colour – that is actually being racist. I need allies to do the work to be anti-racist and do what they can to advance and support Black people.

Many organizations partner with BYP to help empower their current Black employees and potentially reach new people who may want to work with them. It is notable how many companies will create a partnership with an organization yet not do the work to actually be inclusive and allow those newly hired Black employees to thrive. I asked Kike how a partnership with an organization works successfully in practice and how she has used BYP as a way to hold these companies accountable.

> Working with BYP Network is a start. There's three things companies need to work on – recruitment, retention and reputation. Reputation meaning why should someone want to work at your company? And what is your response to there being no people of colour in your senior leadership team? Word of mouth also plays an important role. Black people have to consider all of these different things – 'can I work for this company? Am I going to be comfortable here?' We have to think about whether we stick with what we know or if the grass is actually greener elsewhere for us. Will our CV even get looked at? When employers post on our job board, these are the questions potential Black applicants ask themselves and this is why we help employers enhance their employer brand through events and content showcasing their internal culture.

> The Black Lives Matter movement of 2020 was a great example. Many companies formed statements, many didn't. Some did the bare minimum and posted a Black square on Instagram or Twitter to show solidarity and moved on. This was a key period where everyone was waiting for companies to step up. And for those that have, they have also gotten the Black consumer's money.

> Reputation is very important because you can lose everything when it goes wrong.

Kike's point resounds heavily – organizations being performative is damaging and society is holding these organizations to account. We saw in the wake of this movement, the BBC allowing the n-word to be broadcast twice on TV, with many people then disengaging with the BBC moving forward:

> There are so many examples of very prominent brands getting this wrong – so much so that it feels like clickbait. Black rage is money for someone. [Black rage is the collective response from Black communities when an organization or person implements things that are directly damaging to them – it also fuels lots of clicks and shares online – which is money for those businesses.]
>
> For us, we've made our corporate partners be accountable for their DE&I work. If they do not attempt to make things better, or they do one thing but try to partner with us whilst their Black employees are leaving and protesting them etc, we will not work with them, post their jobs or partner with them. We will not co-sign companies who are not doing the work – as a minimum, going on a DE&I journey.
>
> We expect organizations to spend time reworking their hiring processes to make sure their job criteria are balanced and fair. It must be realistic – many organizations have long lists of 'must have' criteria, yet the people in those roles already don't have those skills. This is another way to gatekeep. Interviewers must have mandatory bias training, otherwise women like me will not be chosen over a white person because I am less relatable.
>
> Additionally, to help organizations get this right, we now have a group of consultants that can provide education on all of these things. First and foremost, we're a tech platform; however, we have a strong network and that is a privilege that we can now use to continue to make an even bigger impact. We suggest to all organizations that they should focus on these five things to make a meaningful difference: 1) bridging the ethnicity pay gap,

2) introducing ally programmes, 3) leveraging internal Black/ BAME networks, 4) working on long-term solutions and 5) individual change.

It's clear working with BYP that Black employees feel more comfortable and a stronger sense of belonging because they feel seen, heard and empowered. That's why it's important for us to keep growing right and be that known platform for all things Black professional. Because of us, we have seen organizations create new employee resource groups for Black or BAME staff and then work with us on really empowering that internal community.

We have seen a rise in Black and multicultural networks being created internally. I asked Kike what a successful employee network looks like. She said:

Your internal network should be the hub where communities can come together, talk about issues, organize internal events and tie in with the recruitment team. They should be paid for their time – through the responsibility being part of their career objectives, meaning it plays a part in their promotion case, through an actual increase in salary or both. It should provide access to new opportunities to hold the organization to account. Too many organizations make statements about how they will double their Black representation in five years' time but then don't update throughout that time. Then it gets near the deadline and a statement is put out that they didn't make it and we have to wait another five years for an update.

Given the increase in Head of/Leadership DE&I roles, I asked Kike's opinion on this. She said:

These roles have to have people who have experience doing DE&I work. It can't just be people who identify with a group. They have to have experience doing this work for it to be really strategic. Organizations also need to know that hiring a Chief

Diversity Officer is not a silver bullet and does not make your organization suddenly diverse. The role is part of a long-term solution. These issues will not change overnight.

Kike makes a very clear point – organizations must be accountable for their efforts and the success or failures of these. Leadership must be aware of how biases play into these potential successes or failures. Regularly, humans group people together with assumed traits and behaviours so as to make shortcut decisions without being entirely overloaded with nuance and information. But this does mean there is a clear and very real opportunity for discrimination, prejudice and bias to be hard-wired into all of our decision making, choices and lifestyles.

What's important is that we continuously:

- recognize when we do these things – *self-awareness*;
- listen and learn from those we have disadvantaged or hurt, remembering to not be defensive – *vulnerability and education*;
- internalize this learning and awareness into our actions – *inclusive action*.

This continuous process is called allyship. Let's chat about how to be an ally.

References

Engler, A (2019) [accessed 13 December 2020] For Some Employment Algorithms, Disability Discrimination by Default, Brookings [Online] www.brookings.edu/blog/techtank/2019/10/31/for-some-employment-algorithms-disability-discrimination-by-default/ (archived at https://perma.cc/7TEM-NGSW)

Ethics Unwrapped (2013) [accessed 13 December 2020] Fundamental Attribution Error: Ethics Unwrapped [Online] https://ethicsunwrapped.utexas.edu/glossary/fundamental-attribution-error (archived at https://perma.cc/7YAX-PRD3)

Gagné, Y (2018) [accessed 13 December 2020] Just 34 Black Women Founders Have Raised Over $1 Million in Venture Funding Since 2009, Inc.com [Online] www.inc.com/yasmin-gagne/just-34-black-women-founders-raised-over-1-million-in-venture-funding-since-2009.html (archived at https://perma.cc/NS66-E9KC)

Grierson, J (2020) [accessed 13 December 2020] Met Carried out 22,000 Searches on Young Black Men During Lockdown, *The Guardian*, 8 July [Online] www.theguardian.com/law/2020/jul/08/one-in-10-of-londons-young-black-males-stopped-by-police-in-may (archived at https://perma.cc/CES9-ASN4)

Guo, A, Kamar, E, Vaughan, JW, Wallach, H and Morris, MR (2020) Toward fairness in AI for people with disabilities, SBG@a research roadmap. ACM SIGACCESS. *Accessibility and Computing*, **125**, article no. 6

Hoffman, KM, Trawalter, S, Axt, JR and Oliver, MN (2016) Racial bias in pain assessment and treatment recommendations, and false beliefs about biological differences between blacks and whites. *Proceedings of the National Academy of Sciences*, **113** (16), pp 4296–4301

Hoffower, H and Borden, T (2019) [accessed 13 December 2020] How Much it Costs to Have a Baby in Every State, Whether you have Health Insurance or Don't, *Business Insider* [Online] www.businessinsider.com/how-much-does-it-cost-to-have-a-baby-2018-4?r=US&IR=T (archived at https://perma.cc/4QB4-RDMH)

Hutchinson, B, Prabhakaran, V, Denton, E, Webster, K, Zhong, Y and Denuyl, S (2020) Unintended machine learning biases as social barriers for persons with disabilities. ACM SIGACCESS, *Accessibility and Computing*, **125** [Online] https://storage.googleapis.com/pub-tools-public-publication-data/pdf/00f5e80a5ba35699fee847b0f564eba016f603b3.pdf (archived at https://perma.cc/U3X2-TYB7)

Jacobs, T (2017) [accessed 13 December 2020] Black Male Faces More Likely to Be Seen as Threatening, *Pacific Standard* [Online] https://psmag.com/economics/black-male-faces-3571 (archived at https://perma.cc/PVB6-VCR7)

Jaschik, S (2014) [accessed 13 December 2020] Study Finds that Faculty Members are More Likely to Respond to White Males than Others [Online] www.insidehighered.com/news/2014/04/24/study-finds-faculty-members-are-more-likely-respond-white-males-others (archived at https://perma.cc/J78A-TEB6)

Kasprzak, E (2019) [accessed 13 December 2020] Why Are Black Mothers at More Risk of Dying? *BBC News*, 11 April [Online] www.bbc.co.uk/news/uk-england-47115305 (archived at https://perma.cc/GT57-YTAQ)

MBRRACE (2016) [accessed 13 December 2020] Maternal, Newborn and Infant Clinical Outcome Review Programme Saving Lives, Improving Mothers' Care [Online] www.npeu.ox.ac.uk/downloads/files/mbrrace-uk/reports/MBRRACE-UK%20Maternal%20Report%202018%20-%20Web%20Version.pdf (archived at https://perma.cc/V8C2-TLRY)

Sippitt, A (2015) [accessed 13 December 2020] Job Applicants with Ethnic Minority Sounding Names are Less Likely to be Called for Interview, *Full Fact* [Online] https://fullfact.org/economy/job-applicants-ethnic-minority-sounding-names-are-less-likely-be-called-interview/ (archived at https://perma.cc/ABM3-D3J9)

CHAPTER SIX

Stand up

Being an ally

This chapter will focus on:

- What is an ally?
- What is allyship?
- What is performative allyship vs actionable allyship?
- Top tips on being a better ally

To ally is to combine and work together (personally or systemi-cally) for a common and mutual benefit. A joining of two forces to create a benefit for all. When we understand how we can combine our strengths, shortcomings and experiences, we can actively make a difference to how society works for people like us and people who are not like us. This is not complicated, but it is incredibly effective.

Being an ally and allyship are key to unlocking the power of diversity. To have the most successful and well-rounded world and society, representation of marginalized groups in industry must improve. To invoke this change, the majority must help, support and advocate for the minority. If engaged correctly, allies hold the power and the key to stimulate positive change. It is unfair and close to impossible for marginalized and underrepresented people to shift the narrative and create a fairer society when they are already underrepresented in the rooms where decisions are made and are actively listened to less than those from majority groups because of the dilution of their assimilation and closeness to power. Think about it – how difficult is it to change anything in any realm of life if you have no say or power to do so – or if you're not close to someone who does wield that power? This is where allyship comes in as a way to level a very bumpy and uneven playing field.

What is an ally?

An ally is any person who actively promotes and aspires to advance the culture of inclusion through intentional, positive and conscious efforts that benefit people as a whole. Allies should be actively working to help those who they do and do not directly identify with – there is no need to have a direct attachment to care and want a community to have better opportunities.

You do not need to be or know a member of the LGBT+ community to care about LGBT+ rights. You do not need to be or know someone from the Black community to care about Black rights. You do not need to be or know a woman to care about gender-based rights. And so on. We spoke about intersectionality earlier and this is directly relevant to allyship. Everyone has the ability to be an ally as privilege is intersectional – white women can be actionable allies to people of colour, men can be allies to women, cis people can be allies to members of the LGBTQ+ community, non-disabled people can be allies to those with different abilities, economically privileged people can be allies to those who are not and so on.

What is allyship?

Allyship is the direct action of an ally and the specific work done by an ally to learn (or unlearn) the experiences of different communities whilst using their privilege to shift the dial for these groups. I want us to think about performative vs actionable allyship.

When you hear the word 'performative' what do you think of? What other words come to mind? For me, when I think of 'performative', I also think of 'facetious', 'self-serving' and 'disingenuous'. These words can directly be used to describe performative allyship. It isn't about actually helping underrepresented communities. The focus is actually on the ally being rewarded and getting benefits from being 'one of the good ones' whilst doing the bare minimum.

What is performative allyship vs actionable allyship?

Performative allyship is rooted in only allowing for change that is comfortable or 'accepted' by the majority group. This involves:

- *Tone policing* – 'don't be too aggressive with your words. That's not very nice', therefore disregarding the hurt and emotion, only to accept a certain type of engagement that centres the perpetrator over the victim. A good example of this is how society talks about racism. Consider how many times you'll have heard about people calling out racism being told that they can't say that something is racist etc, vs actually focusing on the racism being perpetuated.
- *Palatable engagement* – this is doing the bare minimum to appear caring and engaged. Performative allyship is rooted in self-service and getting praise for being an ally (the antithesis of true allyship). An example of this is in the global uproar

after George Floyd's murder at the hands of the police in 2020, when many people and organizations spent one day posting a single black square on their social media to 'stand in solidarity with the Black community', whilst using the hashtag #BlackLivesMatter. There are a number of things here that aren't useful. Firstly, from a practical standpoint, using the #BlackLivesMatter hashtag with no actual content meant that useful posts with petition links and educational content were pushed down 'explore' pages, meaning they weren't being found when they were most needed. Secondly, posting a black square is all well and good but what else are you doing? Anti-Blackness is internalized deeply into our society and posting a black square doesn't address that. Sure, showing solidarity in this way may have a point, but it is certainly not the start and finish of our work. If you post a square but don't spend time learning about the history that has brought us to this moment, sign petitions, keep talking and educating your white and non-Black friends and family and donating (if you can), then you are being performative.

- *Personal attachment as a necessity* – allyship and caring about other people should not require any direct or indirect connection. Do you need to know a gay person to care about gay rights? Do you need to have disabled people amongst your friends or family to care about disabled rights? Simply – no. We must understand that we should use our privilege for all people, regardless of whether their betterment directly benefits us (or the people we care about) or not. Because of this type of allyship, we have seen that most diversity and inclusion efforts have positively affected white, non-disabled, cisgendered, heterosexual, economically privileged women. Because white men in leadership can ultimately identify with white women more than any other minority group.

So, what does genuine empowering and impactful allyship look like?

Top tips on being a better ally

To be an ally, your words and action must be in sync. Words without actions are detrimental and work against changing an exclusive culture. If we say one thing, yet do another that directly contradicts this, then what are we doing other than being self-serving and causing further hurt and damage? Here are my top tips on being a better ally.

Recognize and actively seek out learning on systemic inequalities

WHY?

We cannot understand how to be an ally if we don't actually understand what we're trying to address and readdress. It's impossible to know where to go if you don't know where you've been. It's also crucial to recognize the exclusions and exclusiveness that have happened that may not have actively affected you but have had detrimental effects on others. A 'head in the sand' approach is of no use to anyone as it falls back to being performative. If we want to care and make changes for the better, we must understand and accept what society has done previously. This might mean that you find out things that you are uncomfortable with, and that there are people you idolize that actually should have been held to account (think Susan B. Anthony and the Suffragettes that we spoke about earlier, or about the impact of the British Empire and colonization on the world). This is a journey and we must accept that everything we know will not have always been the entire story.

HOW THIS WORKS IN PRACTICE

Personally, you should seek out education on the history that has brought us to the bias-led society we now live in. Google is free. Do not rely on marginalized people to educate you. Start by deciding what your aims are and why. Let's use the example of Black inequity.

Start by understanding the history of how Black people have been treated – learning about slavery, police brutality, the Windrush generation, employment rates and housing income inequities, and how the Covid-19 pandemic is disproportionately affecting marginalized communities. This is a marathon so pace yourself. Set a promise that you will read and digest at a minimum one piece a week/fortnight. Start to follow some well-known DE&I leaders who regularly post trustworthy information so you can trust what you're reading without being overwhelmed. Or ask those in your organization what they read to help further their own knowledge.

Then, start to delve into what it means to be Black right now in today's society – learning about hiring bias, policing of Black bodies and hair, the differing prison sentences depending on how dark you are, the intersection of socioeconomic background and ethnicity, and more. Again, remember this is a journey and treat this education as something that you incorporate into your life – you don't just read one article or book and finish.

Now, you need to start understanding how to be actively anti-racist and to support ways creating a more equitable environment – regularly donating, educating your family members (and holding them to account), teaching your children to be anti-racist, discussing this in the workplace and bringing this new education to light in a way that effects change.

If you're in a position to, hire or create anti-racism learning resources for your workplace so people can access, educate and rework their thinking to create a wave of practical allyship.

Realize the impact of micro-aggressions

Micro-aggressions are everyday actions, verbal and non-verbal whether intentional or unintentional, that are hostile or derogatory against a specific person or group because of their identity, race, gender, disability and so on. Examples are the constant mispronunciation of someone's name (which is non-Western), regularly confusing people of the same ethnicity, describing disabled people as 'inspirational', making assumptions about people's preferences based on their sexuality, saying that someone seems very smart for a Black person etc. If these things do not happen to you, hearing that they do occur may seem like no big deal. But that assumption doesn't take into account the regularity of these occurrences and how 'small' things have a big impact on people when they continually happen. Death by a thousand cuts is a very real thing – if you had one of those small cuts and none after, you'd probably be ok, but when you have thousands of them, that is a different story.

HOW THIS WORKS IN PRACTICE

Again, education plays an important role here. If you haven't experienced micro-aggressions you won't know what they are and their impact. Spend time reading up on the type of micro-aggressions that are present in the world, then consider if they're present in your workplace (they will be!). You'll see reference to many micro-aggressions in the Privilege Walk exercise you did earlier.

Next up, incorporate dealing with micro-aggressions into your workplace DNA. Micro-aggressions will exist and it's your job to help those suffering from them (remember that emotional tax we just spoke about?). Review your grievance policy in the way we spoke about in the first chapter, provide mandatory education on micro-aggressions and their impact firstly to senior leadership then mid-management and then the rest of the organization (a tiered approach is more scalable and allows you to get decision makers on board first). Determine appropriate action for those who are repeatedly called out for perpetuating micro-aggressions and have mental health first-aiders appropriately trained to deal with those suffering.

Believe experiences of those who are underrepresented

There are things you will hear that will be shocking and almost impossible for you to comprehend. The reason for that is privilege and an ability to not have been affected in the same way. Instead of immediately reacting (inwardly or outwardly) with 'I can't believe that', 'There's no way that happened', 'You're over-reacting, it was just a comment' or 'That doesn't sound like something I've ever heard before', consider *why* this is your immediate reaction. Humans are multifaceted and have all different experiences – it's highly unlikely that one person will have fully experienced every single issue, and that's why listening is important. Remember that there is a difference between listening to speak and listening to learn. When we are listening to speak, we're simply allowing someone else to speak and not digesting what they're saying, because we're mentally preparing to say our rebuttal or to state something else that was relevant to the conversation prior to the new statements from the person speaking. We're not actually really listening. When we're listening to learn, we are listening, digesting and analysing what the person is saying before creating our own response. We're also spending the time to listen, even when the statements may counteract our own beliefs. We need this kind of listening from allies to underrepresented groups.

HOW THIS WORKS IN PRACTICE

This kind of listening must be embedded into your organization's culture, through the data you capture, how you facilitate listening sessions across different groups and how leadership responds. You can have one-to-one listening sessions and you should also have a system in place for employees to answer engagement questions about how they view inclusion, progression and belonging in your organization. These questions should be able to be split across demographics, otherwise you can't listen to experiences properly. For example, if you see that 75 per cent of your organization has a sense of belonging, but 80 per cent of your employees are white, are you truly understanding if your non-white employees are feeling that same sense of belonging? If people share and nothing happens, you have caused extra harm after someone has gone through the emotional toil of sharing.

There are times when this will be hard for you, but remember how much harder it has been for those who have not been listened to or actively included by the majority.

Advocate for others by sponsoring their work and achievements

Champion someone from an underrepresented community to support career growth and increase company retention. Being a sponsor is different from being a mentor – sponsoring is being actively involved in aiding someone's career progression; mentoring is providing advice. According to research from the Center for Talent Innovation:

> [t]he vast majority of women (85%) and multicultural professionals (81%) need navigational support to advance in their careers but receive it less often than Caucasian men. However, a 2010 Catalyst study revealed that more women than men have been assigned mentors yet 15% more men won promotions. Why? The findings indicate that having more mentorship did not lead to advancement but having a senior mentor in a position to provide sponsorship did. (Stanford, 2014).

Sponsorship is actively getting involved in someone's progression – giving them visibility when they're not in the room, giving them constructive feedback because people cannot progress with just positive feedback (we need to know what we can do better too!) and actively seeking out opportunities for them. Constructive feedback is a crucial part of sponsorship. Analysis of over

200 performance reviews by *Harvard Business Review* has shown that reviews for women have less useful and more vague praise more often than reviews for men (57 per cent and 43 per cent, respectively). Comments like 'You had a great year' was regularly present in women's reviews. In contrast, the analysis found that developmental feedback for men was more likely to be linked to business outcomes (60 per cent for men versus 40 per cent for women) (Correll and Simard, 2016). Like I said, you cannot progress if you don't know what you can do better. Feedback plays a gear-shifting role here.

HOW THIS WORKS IN PRACTICE

This requires a framework as part of this initiative. Do not roll out an informal network as it will favour those who are more confident and self-aware than those who are not. There must be a framework to create a baseline expectation and understanding for all involved. A successful sponsorship framework should include:

- Clearly defined mission – why are you doing this and who is it for? What is the target group? Women and people of colour? Women of colour? Other underrepresented groups? What part of the business? What levels etc?
- A curated list of sponsors – sponsors should be senior leadership or people with decision-making abilities to be able to properly advocate, detail how to progress to their level and provide visibility for sponsees. Appropriate training and do's and don'ts should be provided to sponsors as not all senior leadership is aware of how to be a sponsor. This should include a checklist of questions to fall back on if needs be, information on how to help with do's and don'ts on how to talk to and about your sponsee.
- A list of sponsees – There are a number of ways to do this. You can either have:
  - Self-nominations – allow people to nominate themselves by sharing a number of questions for them to answer such as

'why do you believe you would benefit from a sponsor?', 'what are your career goals and how do you think you will reach them?' alongside a number of self-rating questions on confidence, responsibilities and decision making. After this, a facilitator and the pool of sponsors should sit down and define who takes part and why. Clear criteria must be used here to avoid bias seeping in. Criteria may be around tenure in organization alongside how long they have been at their level (if it's longer than expected, they may need some support), with queries such as 'are they recognized as a high performer or show potential to be?', 'do they have the potential to develop their career?', 'would they benefit from profile raising?' and 'have they discussed career aspirations and need assistance in reaching them?' Work should be done to encourage junior/mid-tier eligible employees to put themselves forward – again, we do not want to disadvantage those who may be less confident in doing so.

- Selected sponsees – this will involve incorporating the opportunity to be part of your talent review process, having managers make a note of who they believe could benefit from this kind of programme. After this has been done, similar criteria to the above should be used to define who takes part (as you may have too many potential sponsees). One way to avoid too many sponsees is to define X number of sponsors per business unit and then allocate the same number of sponsee spaces, so there is no issue with numbers.

- Defined feedback cycle – for a sponsorship programme to be successful, there must be a constant feedback loop between sponsor and sponsee. This should start off by asking all sponsees to complete a survey capturing their self-ratings, the areas they believe they need support in and the areas they believe they're strong in. This initial feedback report should be provided to sponsors ahead of time to ensure the first conversation is fruitful. After the programme kicks off, similar surveys should be sent at least every two months so sponsees can detail any changes in their confidence/work and the facilitator can see any growing trends whilst also being able to address any issues if need be.

- Templated materials for sponsees – sponsees need to be provided with development trackers and an initial one-pager to complete on their strengths, growth areas, things they do and don't enjoy working on etc. The development tracker should be a spreadsheet that allows them to track each of their goals with corresponding deadlines, actions taken, skills/ knowledge needed/gaps to fill, what help they need to make it happen and why, what does success look like to them and their progress. This should be shared with their sponsor in each meeting.

- Defined sponsor/sponsee meeting expectations – the creation of these meetings is the responsibility of the sponsee and they should be at a minimum once a month, where they discuss progress against development tracker, any issues the sponsee has had and any meetings/opportunities the sponsor has access to share. Whilst a template should be provided, it should also be respected that people will find a flow that works for them too and any of these new ideas or ways of working should be captured in the feedback cycle so they can potentially be rolled out wider if they're useful.

- Defined timelines – transparency is inclusion 101. Everyone should be on the same page at all times. Set a programme length (usually 6–12 months) that is in line with your promotion cycle as, ultimately, the goal of the programme is to see more underrepresented people promoted.

In every organization I have worked in, I have defined and rolled out a sponsorship framework. I now have a template that I use that I tailor depending on the organization and it allows me to roll out an impactful initiative relatively quickly.

Eventually, once the organization is aware of what sponsorship is and how it should work (I suggest running the programme once or twice to capture this feedback for tweaking), sponsorship should be baked into part of leadership and management progression. When you reach a certain level, the support of junior/mid-tier growth and progression is part of your role. This programme should still exist to ensure underrepresented people are not unconsciously forgotten about.

Share growth opportunities

At certain points in our careers, we will start to get regular opportunities and new assignments because of our seniority levels. There are times when we know that there are people who could really benefit from these opportunities to grow, learn and develop. More often than not, these opportunities are allocated to people similar to us. Now, if the majority of people in leadership are white, straight, men, then who is more likely to get the new growth opportunities? And so, the cycle continues. If you do this, a part of allyship will be actively spending time analysing who you think of right away for opportunities and why. The 'why' is important – are there certain skills you always think of that you know person X has? Do you judge the person on previous experience or on potential? Are these people similar to you and, therefore, likely to create something similar to you in some way? Now, think about the groups of people you may not be considering. That's why this is a continuous conversation. People slip back into habits – it's human nature. True allyship disrupts this, making sure that we regularly check the different exclusionary systemic processes we either feed into or benefit from.

HOW THIS WORKS IN PRACTICE

Opportunity sharing leads to a more equitable environment because it spreads the load of who gets the opportunity to be exceptional and excel. Almost everyone has the ability to be exceptional, but do they all have the opportunity? Keep track of who you are giving opportunities to in a spreadsheet, detail who they are, why you've given them the opportunity and the impact you hope they have. Review this every month/quarter/bi-annually and see if you note any trends. If you do, make a point of actively disrupting your decision on who gets what before you allocate it. Hold yourself to account on this.

Be proactive about supporting underrepresented people

Don't wait for someone to reach out for help. Reach out to them and ask if you can help them. Note if you see them struggling to speak up in meetings or be heard – proactively say to the room that you want to hear from them. If there is something happening in the world that you know will have affected them personally, reach out and offer your support. Help them get growth opportunities without them having to ask for your help.

Understand that you reaching out takes the burden off these people to always reach out for help.

HOW THIS WORKS IN PRACTICE

This is simple. You reach out, ask and share how you think you can help. Never assume someone needs your help as they may not want it. Remember to not be upset or get frustrated if they say they don't want your help. And do not let this deter you from reaching out to others who may still want your help. This isn't about you and do not put yourself at the centre or as the main focus.

Hold yourself (and those around you) accountable

Accountability is key. All words, no action makes for performative allyship. We will mess up and we will get things wrong, myself included. No one is perfect. With this in mind, we must have checks in place to catch us when we slip up and have a method of moving forward. We have to understand that when we slip up, even if unintentionally, it will and can still cause pain and hurt to other people. Remember, intention and impact are two very different things and, as allies, we must prioritize the impact on underrepresented people.

It's very easy to jump headfirst straight into allyship, committing to doing lots and lots of things and then getting overwhelmed and doing nothing. Remember again, in the wake of George Floyd's murder, for several weeks we had non-Black people posting outrage etc; however, after a month or two, this quietened down and they went back to their lives. Listen and watch for signs of performative allyship in yourself and others.

HOW THIS WORKS IN PRACTICE

To ensure this doesn't happen with you, when you commit to something, add in touchpoints to check how you are getting on (with yourself). For example, can you commit to reading one or two anti-racism pieces per week and discussing them with family members across a month? Can you set up a regular donation (if financially able) to a charity that is working to help the group that you want to create a better environment for? Can you keep a log of who you give opportunities to, then review it at the end of a monthly/quarterly period to see if you've actually put into practice disrupting this systemic inequity? If you're in leadership and you make organization commitments, how often are you checking in with how progress is going (either through employee engagement surveys or the data of your employee base)? Keeping a check on how you personally are seeing through the things you're committing to is key.

When watching for performative allyship in others, watch out for tell-tale signs such as:

- Using the phrase 'culture fit' – expecting someone to blend in or match a certain way of working that works for you and some of your employees but is making an assumption that you *have* to work that way to work there.
- Making any assumptions on what anyone wants without having spoken to them first. For example, assuming that

caregivers don't want a promotion because it means more travel, where the assumption is that they can't travel.

- Centring the perpetrator over the victim. When someone has had something happen to them and the immediate reaction is 'Oh, I'm sure they didn't mean any harm' or 'That definitely doesn't sound like something X would do'. Remember, believe underrepresented people's experiences.

- Saying things like 'you/they are just being too sensitive'. Like I said before, what may not be a big impact on you can be on others and it's important to hold each other to account when this happens. Remind people about why this is an impact for other people and commit to learning and not repeating the same mistake.

- Rating some people using potential and others with performance. This is important to watch for in sponsorship because, typically, we see majority demographic people being reviewed on potential and underrepresented people on previous performance. This is usually because we have majority demographic people in leadership positions, who therefore can 'see themselves' or similarities to themselves/those around them in other people like them, and therefore can envision their success because, well, other people like them were good at it so why wouldn't these people be good too? If people are doing this but don't believe they are, analyse your performance process data to see who was promoted, who applied and wasn't, and the tenure/experience of those people.

But what happens if you slip up or your efforts fall short? Transparency and honesty are key here. If you do not actively make the changes you've stated you'll make, or you realize you've fallen back into old habits, spend time thinking about why this is. It is likely because it is easier and more comfortable for you to do this and, therefore, you've slipped back. Additionally, if you say something that someone tells you is offensive or just not quite right, remember not to be defensive. This is a learning journey and what you can do is listen to their reasoning, apologize and move forward noting this new information. Be thankful when someone does this for you too – your education is no one else's responsibility but your own. Make sure you do not expect or ask the group you're aiming to help to keep a check on you – this is not their job and your learning journey is not their job.

When you put all of these things together, remember that this is a continuous process.

Practical allyship

Putting this into practice takes time and awareness but has a significant impact.

HOW THIS WORKS IN PRACTICE

Putting your money where your mouth is   In 2020, Alexis Ohanian, the founder and former CEO of Reddit (a social news aggregation, web content rating and discussion website), stepped down from his position on the company's board in response to the protests against police brutality after Minneapolis police killed George Floyd, an unarmed Black man. Alexis is married to Serena Williams, who needs no introduction, and they have a daughter together. After George Floyd was murdered and his story hit headlines, Ohanian penned a Twitter thread saying he had to be able to answer his Black daughter on 'what did you do' to make things better. When he resigned he urged the Board to fill his seat with a Black candidate and made a commitment to use all future gains on his Reddit stock to serve the Black community, starting with a US $1 million pledge to Your Rights Camp, a free campaign for youth funded by Colin Kaepernick to raise awareness on self-empowerment and interacting with law enforcement (Hatmaker and Lunden, 2020).

Using your voice or brand for influence   We don't all have millions to donate, but we do have a voice or a desired way to communicate. In 2020, Matt Wallaert, a well-known Behavioural scientist in the tech industry and author of *Start At The End*, a guide to creating products that create change, publicly called out that he was aware of a company that had specifically laid off their white men employees with substantial severance packages, yet didn't give women and people of colour this option, keeping them whilst increasing their workload and cutting their pay. He gave them a week to respond, with constant follow-ups and reaching out to their legal team but no response came. At the end of this deadline, he went public with a thread sharing that company named Toast, alongside proof of what they'd done and more (Wallaert, 2010). I spoke to Matt to understand his aims behind this very public (potentially personally risky) approach and he said:

> I wanted them to correct the situation. To me, that was a
> very simple thing: offer all retained employees the ability to
> take the same severance package as those Toast involuntarily
> terminated. What happened was... not that. It wasn't for lack
> of trying. I wrote to investors. I [even] wrote to board members.
> I followed up on social media. Hell, I even pulled in favours
> to get the personal email address of some of the founders and
> wrote to them. And here we are – they're all doing just fine,
> they aren't repentant.

This thread went viral in the tech community, with many prominent leaders picking it up; however, this story is not an anomaly. It could be argued that what Matt did was very risky and could have put his own personal livelihood at risk. I asked him if he considered this a real risk to him (as a white man in tech, with a well-known reputation) and he said:

> No. Not because it isn't possible that saying something publicly
> hurt my chances of getting a future position or annoyed some

people. But part of privilege is knowing that I will always be able to get a job. The whole reason that Toast employees didn't want to sue or do something publicly is because they didn't have the same certainty of re-employment. That's the real tragedy.

I think often of the line from *Romeo and Juliet*: 'My poverty, not my will, consents.' That is the reality of work for so many people: it is bad, but they don't feel they have options. And so because I do have options, I'm not simply going to stand here quietly.

True allyship is putting yourself in the line for others because you have the serious awareness that you know you can and others cannot. You're willing to take this risk. Given Matt's very public stance in this situation and his continued work online in engaging white men as allies, I asked him what top three tips would he give to anyone in a position of privilege to actively work on dismantling the systems that serve so many whilst disadvantaging others. He said:

Change is an active process – nothing changes unless we change it; the status quo bias will keep things as they are unless we put effort into preventing it. So we have to be active agents of change, whether that means creating impediments to what we don't want or finding new ways to motivate what we do.

You can't please everyone – the world isn't zero sum, particularly in the long run. But when we dismantle privilege, that means some people will have fewer privileges than they have enjoyed before and they typically won't give that up willingly. You cannot expect everyone will be happy with what you're doing and trying to keep them happy will only make you less effective.

Know why you're doing it – people, even on 'your side', will question your motives and if you get that often enough, you'll start to question whether it is worth it if you're so misunderstood. To shield yourself, know why you're seeking to dismantle the system and stick to that doggedly; stay connected to your root cause and let your actions flow from it.

Similarly to Ohanian's aim of striving for better board diversity, several countries have been mandating gender diversity for board positions in an aim to level the playing field. In 2008, Norway mandated that all publicly listed companies must reserve at least 40 per cent of their director seats for women. Five years later, several other countries such as Belgium, France and Italy have all set similar mandates, with those not complying being fined, dissolved or banned from paying directors that are currently in position. Other countries have taken a softer approach, with Spain, Germany and the Netherlands opting for soft-law quotas with no repercussions if they are not met. You may be wondering what the UK has done in this scenario? They opted for guidelines and advice (*The Economist*, 2018).

Now, perhaps you don't have the clout to publicly call out a US $5 billion startup or to put new policies into place, but maybe you can do one of these things too.

INTERVENING DAY TO DAY

For me personally, I will actively say the names of those who are not in the rooms I am in, putting them forward for growth opportunities and amplifying their work to make sure they are properly credited. I will call out when I believe someone is being treated/rated harsher than their equivalents and ask for very clear reasoning – if I don't get it, I will keep pushing until decisions are reversed or people admit that unfairness is present. As a senior leader, I am inherently privileged because I am listened to and that is one of the biggest privileges of all.

Alongside work-related allyship, I will actively insert myself into conversations to protect Black women having to go through the emotional exhaustion of responding to deliberately aggressive or wilfully ignorant conversations. I have the privilege to do so. Likewise, if I see people from the LGBTQ+ community being harassed, I step in. If I'm in an environment where I think someone isn't being treated fairly or properly, I will insert myself into the conversation to ask why someone is asking what they're asking or can they clarify why they think that is ok. I will do this with people I know and people I don't.

I actively donate to the support of those who need it. I am not wealthy but I am comfortable enough to be able to share expendable income. Just like you, I am on a journey of allyship.

Here are some phrases you can use if you hear something that doesn't feel acceptable or fair:

- *Tell me why you said that* – ask for clarification and put the onus on the person to share why they said it. If they shrug it off or can't give an answer, make it clear that it wasn't ok and why.
- *I don't get it – is there a reason you have thought this was funny? Can you explain it to me?* – hearing jokes that are offensive and seeking a clear answer on why it's funny will mean someone will have to be honest about the group they're content with offending, which usually creates an awkward, learning moment. Be comfortable with this awkwardness.
- *We don't do this here* – this is a powerful statement as there is no discussion as to why the behaviour isn't acceptable. It simply reaffirms that within this workplace/environment etc, that we don't do that here. The first time I heard this was from Jonas Templestein, CTO and Co-Founder at Monzo Bank, and it has stayed with me since.

Allyship is a continuous journey and I cannot stress that enough. We must have a feedback loop with ourselves:

- Recognize when we do things or benefit from systems that actively disadvantage others – *self-awareness.*
- Listen and learn from those we have disadvantaged or hurt, remembering to not be defensive – *vulnerability and education.*
- Internalize this learning and awareness into our actions – *inclusive action.*

Allyship is a tool to make a crucial impact in inclusion, using your own personal privilege and clout to advance society for those you do and do not identify with. There was no better person for me to discuss this with than Kate Robertson, the Co-founder of One Young World and ex Havas. One Young World is the global forum for young leaders that sees over 1,400 delegates from 196 countries each year attend, with luminaries such as Kofi Annan, Professor Muhammad Yunus, Sir Bob Geldof, Paul Polman and Arianna Huffington in attendance. Prior to One Young World, Kate was the Global President and UK Group Chairman of Havas Worldwide, where she was the highest placed woman in the advertising industry worldwide. Kate's experience spans almost 40 years and she has dedicated her career to societal change through empowering, advocating and promoting the next generation of leaders.

Given the global footprint of One Young World and its influence, I asked Kate about the privilege (or power) that comes with leading an organization like this and how has she utilized this for good, to create a more inclusive society. She said:

> Do I think One Young World has power as a non-profit organization? Potentially no, it has taken years to get some of our luminaries; however, that has given us a lot of privilege. These powerful people being involved with us has given us a lot of privilege, by association. In this balance, I have a concomitant duty. If I have a privilege, I have a responsibility. To get to this position, I had to be very clear on what our first line was – our real mission. It was about the search and promotion of young leaders from every country in the world. Our next step was then to think about the responsibilities concomitant on that. They were 1) the inclusion of women and people of colour, 2) being clear on what we have been successful with and 3) being clear on what we still needed to do. You have to be aware that with this great responsibility, you cannot fix everything overnight (and sometimes that thought

is devastating). Because as much progress as is made, you will always feel like 'oh my god, we've made 99 per cent progress – but what about the final 1 per cent!' To truly embrace this responsibility, you need to have rigour with yourself because if you try to do everything, you will get nowhere.

Given One Young World's mission is quite literally to find and empower young leaders, I asked Kate how she sees young leaders creating more inclusive environments (and how young leaders in your own organization should be empowered). She said:

Young people have a combination of health (if they are lucky, this isn't a given), energy, hope and time. With this mix, there is an ability to push (and keep pushing) for real change around inclusion, climate change, politics, you name it. I have three things I always say to support young leaders:

1 *Empower them* – watch them and their work and actively advocate for them when you can. The older generation that sits in leadership has the ears of many and it's their turn to start making sure they are not the only ones listened to.

2 *Listen to them* – I see too many organizations promoting having 'young voices at the table', but what that really means is have it covered with young 'token people' and do not actually give them any time or responsibility. This does no one any service. Bring these people in but only if you are willing to be challenged. Otherwise, do not bother wasting their time and using them as a fig leaf for inaction. What I'd also say to young people is do not allow anyone to use you as a token representative. Don't go to an event unless you're an official delegate, or you have appropriate measures in place to ensure that you'll be able to raise your concerns. Your time is worth more than that.

3 *Hold them accountable* – young people are people. They deserve to be held to a standard to allow them to grow with continuous constructive feedback. No one knows everything

and a true older leader will surround a young leader with support and useful feedback, otherwise, a young person cannot understand how they can be even better than they are right now.

Kate's experience as a senior woman in industry shines through. It is so evident that she has dedicated her career through the creation of One Young World to advocating and allying the younger next generation of leaders. I spent time with Kate and One Young World after the death of George Floyd at the hands of police brutality in the summer of 2020 to discuss how the organization should and could step up for Black communities globally, given its reach. I asked Kate about what the organization has done and will do for this movement. She said:

> As a white woman, you helped me a lot because I was very anxious at the time – both as an organization and personally. I wanted to get this right. I had seen many organizations rush out a statement, and some have gone on to address their employment practices; however, not many of them. Now, I'm not saying this is an easy thing to do; however, sharing your employment numbers is a simple action. For us, I wanted to make sure we were not centring ourselves as white people. Because it's not relevant. I also didn't want to donate and do nothing else:
>
> • Our first step was listening (which you told me to do). We sat down with all of our staff that were people of colour then also did listening sessions with our white staff as well. Staff shared their stories, particularly on discrimination they've faced in their lives, and we had to listen and understand. This was difficult for people but it was very necessary to know that this kind of action isn't always far away – it is happening to your team mate, colleague.
> • Our second step was then putting this into action. We started running 'Table Talks' that bring together industry leaders (such as yourself and people like Verna Myers, VP of

Inclusion at Netflix) to discuss anti-racism and share best practices with the OYW community and its partners. We were able to use our global connections to get and push out much needed education.

- Our third step was to take the time to understand how we could utilize OYW from a policy perspective. We have ambassadors all over the world and we knew we could do more than listening, donating and educating. For example, we're currently looking at how our ambassadors in the UK can contribute to the root and branch reform of the criminal justice system being conducted in Parliament and the House of Lords. We are also working with Lewis Hamilton's Foundation as they review the work of previous enquiries into systemic racism and towards inclusion of Black people in engineering programmes, along with interviewing him on his thoughts on how we can all be anti-racist.

I believe education is a very serious and important point in inclusion. I think you can educate yourself by hearing the experiences from people who suffer prejudice. But we also learn by reading history itself. And history is written by the victors with colonialism and violence regularly omitted. We must question the written history, how it is taught in schools and who teaches it. There will always be different lenses on the same story. I believe young people like you have a real ability to push for these changes, and I will be there supporting, allying and advocating wherever you need me.

Kate touched on it herself, but given she is a white woman in a senior leadership position globally, I asked her about how she has actively gone on a journey of understanding her own personal privilege and how she has effectively used this privilege to help those who do not have it. She said:

It has been a very long journey and continues to be. I am a white South African and I was certainly aware of that privilege when I went to university in 1974. I was certainly aware of privilege because if you were white in South Africa it was also very easy to get into a good university that would cost extremely little. No Black people were allowed to go to my university in those days. Also, consider those who were economically disadvantaged. Who was going to pay for them to go? No one.

I hate to say it, but my parents were old-fashioned colonialist racist white people and I had to spend a lot of time actively pushing against this mindset when I was growing up. When I realized going to university was a privilege, I also realized how much of a privilege it was to know I would walk out of university to get a job. Yes, I've worked myself to the bone, but I still have the privilege of a first-class education that didn't cost my parents a fortune. If you were born white in South Africa, you had privilege that you and I wouldn't recognize in most countries in the world. That's how privilege works, which of course, is a direct byproduct of legalized prejudice.

To recognize your own privilege, you must be able to have empathy for others. The industry I worked in was extremely materialistic and leaders lacked an ability to have empathy or even sympathy with others because they were too focused on themselves and their possessions. When you realize those things don't matter, you have time to focus on the things that really matter. From an ethnicity perspective, I don't know if you can ever, as a white person, empathize with people of colour, because how can you? You can never be in their shoes or in those situations. You can and should sympathize and understand your role in creating that pain though.

Many leaders will talk about 'putting themselves in other people's shoes' to understand what it means to be someone else. However, on many occasions, this doesn't translate to further action. It remains platitudes that are of no benefit to anyone other than themselves. I asked Kate what she has done from a practical actionable view to put this awareness into meaningful impact. She said:

> From a practical perspective, when organizing the first One Young World summit in 2009, we had people asking about our gender balance for delegates. We had 51 per cent women delegates that year. But what we didn't have was Black people – namely African people. We needed to do more and as a white woman, I had to be clear about how we were going to include these different communities. I worked with the Dutch Ministry of Foreign Affairs, the European Commission and others to make sure we could support delegates from all different countries. In 2012, in Pittsburgh, we made a deliberate effort to reach out to and have delegates from all of the Pacific Island nations because they are so readily forgotten about on global stages.
>
> Moving forward, with corporations who partner with us, we almost always have a good gender balance. Now, we strongly suggest and advise them to prioritize ethnic diversity too because it is not inclusive otherwise. It isn't acceptable to send an entirely white delegation. With other areas of inclusion, such as disability, we need to do more. We're still fighting that fight.
>
> When it comes to the counsellors for example, it is difficult. I have always felt that our only way with this is to be clear and to be transparent. We have approximately 65 per cent of our young leaders coming from the corporate sector and they want to hear from CEOs (not middle management). CEO groups are notoriously un-diverse, with the FTSE 500 being primarily men and primarily white men at that. We have to be willing to spend the time to actively seek leaders inside and outside of those groups. We have had phenomenal counsellors like Desmond Tutu and Kofi Annan and they have brought so much to us.

Because I am senior, I am asked regularly to tap into my network for speakers and well-known experts. I also have to make sure I don't just recommend more white people or white women like me. I have that responsibility to widen this pool.

Leading on from this, I asked Kate about the bias she may have faced in her own career, despite being a privileged white South African. As a senior woman in the industry, being the highest-placed woman in marketing at one stage, I wanted to dig into her own personal experiences. I asked if she had ever faced bias herself. She said:

> I was in that industry for so long and working myself literally to a standstill – working harder than anybody else. But I was raised by a mother who was a professional and she was the first woman on a board in South Africa. Her attitude was that 'Yes, you will have to be better than the men and just get on with it'. So that's what I did. I didn't truly understand the enormous bias that women actually face. I just thought I needed to get on with it, not blame men and get on with it. However, as I moved through my career, I could see and knew the bias was there.

> When I came to Britain in 1986, as a white South African I had prejudice against me and rightly so because of where I was from. Like I said already, I had to spend a lot of time making sure people knew I wasn't racist and that I wasn't the type of person they thought I was. When I got a job in an agency, I was winning millions of sales each month, whilst men around me were in much better jobs and on much higher salaries than me. Really, I thought people were treating me differently because they didn't personally like me – but once I started to work with David [Jones, fellow OYW co-founder and ex-Havas], I realized it was others that were biased towards me because of my gender and I wasn't 'acceptable enough' to be in those rooms. I spent a lot of time as the only woman in the boardroom, in the leadership teams and more.

Kate has clearly spent a lot of her career as an actionable ally, but given her career I asked her if she has had any prominent allies that have made a difference to her personally and what they did to make this difference. She said:

> David Jones has been my biggest supporter and ally. I would say he's more than an ally, he's a champion of mine. I went to Havas as the Executive Vice President for Europe. And he was the global business director. Three years later, he became the Global CEO. He had seen my work first hand and when he became the Global CEO, he made me the Group Chairwoman of UK businesses, which at the time were 13 companies and was easily the third largest chunk at Havas. Many of his colleagues didn't like this, resented him and me and didn't respect me at the start. But David was clear on his support and how I was the decision maker for him. At times, men would go above me to David if they didn't like a decision I made and his response was always 'Whatever Kate has said is what my decision is'. He really does genuinely believe and prove to himself that women are equally as good and often better.

It is clear from both Kate's experiences and from David who has been a meaningful ally to her that a true ally must regularly create a space in their lives to listen to those around them (from the same and different backgrounds), be open to adapting their thinking, actively rework what they believe to be correct (being open to this is one thing, but you have to see it through) and become comfortable being uncomfortable.

References

Correll, S and Simard, C (2016) [accessed 13 December 2020] Research: Vague Feedback is Holding Women Back, *Harvard Business Review* [Online] https://hbr.org/2016/04/research-vague-feedback-is-holding-women-back (archived at https://perma.cc/4TL6-2HG8)

Hatmaker, T and Lunden, I (2020) [accessed 13 December 2020] Alexis Ohanian Steps Down from Reddit Board, Asks for His Seat to Go to a Black Board Member [Online] https://techcrunch.com/2020/06/05/alexis-ohanian-steps-down-reddit-board/ (archived at https://perma.cc/NDM2-AEQR)

Stanford (2014) [accessed 13 December 2020] The Key Role of Sponsorship [Online] https://inclusion.slac.stanford.edu/sites/inclusion.slac.stanford.edu/files/The_Key_Role_of_a_Sponsorship_for_Diverse_Talent.pdf (archived at https://perma.cc/83DW-RDJ4)

The Economist (2018) [accessed 13 December 2020] Ten Years on From Norway's Quota for Women on Corporate Boards [online] www.economist.com/business/2018/02/17/ten-years-on-from-norways-quota-for-women-on-corporate-boards (archived at https://perma.cc/S9AC-LACW)

Wallaert, M (2010) [accessed 13 December 2020] Tweet from Matt Wallaert Calling for Transparency [online] https://twitter.com/mattwallaert/status/1275107695763189761 (archived at https://perma.cc/8PL2-66A5)

CHAPTER SEVEN

Demanding more from our leaders

This chapter will focus on:

- The role of leadership in successful DE&I strategies
- The role of middle management in successful DE&I strategies
- Scaling inclusion efforts as you grow

Leaders play a crucial role in almost every part of your company, so why would diversity and inclusion be any different? Leaders are the people who define your vision and strategy – who bring the company together with one common vision. However, many would define a leader as someone who commands or bosses.

Personally, I take issue with the definition. I dislike the notion of 'commanding' people as there is a difference in leading vs bossing. For me, a leader is someone who provides a unified vision with clear direction, embeds a clear line of two-way communication with their people and delivers both the good and difficult news with empathy. Anyone in leadership not embodying these qualities is a 'boss'. I define a 'boss' as someone who tells you what to do, does not actively seek out feedback from those their decision affects and there is an element of fear or unease to challenging them. Most of us do not want to embody those characteristics and understand that a more empathetic and open leadership and management model makes for better employee experiences and teams.

Leadership are usually those in Head of, Director, VP, C-suite positions who have responsibilities over their remits, with decision-making abilities. These are also usually the people who are involved in promotion, hiring and scaling decisions. To be clear, I believe everyone can embody leadership in any role they are in, but for the sake of clarity on how to engage leadership, I am talking about this specific group in this chapter.

Being in leadership is a privilege and one that people should not take lightly. It means having the ability to push for change and be listened to whilst holding the responsibility of business areas, people and more. Typically, those in leadership positions bring extensive experience, knowledge and insights to allow their organization to make well-defined and complete decisions. It takes time to have the ability to be able to comfortably make decisions in this way, and that only comes with experience and having done something before, researching and actively listening to different perspectives.

The role of leadership in successful DE&I strategies

Leaders have the privilege of the role that they do. Providing direction, insights and advice – and being acutely aware that you will be listened to and amplified – is a privilege. When you know that if or when you speak, the room will go quiet and listen, that is a privilege. Now, the key here is that it is used for the good of others and not just to self-serve. So, why should leadership have a role in the success of DE&I strategies?

Firstly, they are role models of the business. A role model is a person who someone or a group of people admire and whose behaviour they will try to emulate or copy. Leaders, especially those in the C-suite, have this responsibility, whether it is personally desired by them or not. We typically want our leaders to role model good behaviour – inclusive behaviour – but that is not always the case. Realistically, if your CEO communicates brashly, behaves aggressively and takes no notice of their privilege, then the impact on the business is that others will follow suit. Why should they be held to an account that the most senior person in the business isn't? We want the behaviours of senior leaders to be the ones that shape our culture and business in the right direction.

Secondly, they are the decision makers. The power is in their hands in many ways – in the direction the company takes, the products and solutions that are worked on, hiring headcount, the culture they are aiming for and more. With this power, they must decide their thought process before making decisions, otherwise personal bias will potentially creep in. Regardless of that, they play a role in the success of any strategy that touches their remits and DE&I is no different. This decision-making ability means accountability also sits squarely with them – the delivery or lack thereof.

Thirdly, they are influencers. Now maybe you're like me and dislike the word influencer and its meaning in the context of social media, but let's think about how business leaders genuinely influence the wider ecosystem around them. From closed networking events, to prestigious awards and everything in between, business leaders are influencers. We see tech CEOs on the covers of non-tech focused magazines, their stories being pushed across all channels and being consumed by everyone (not just those in the tech sphere). This means that what they do will be watched (and watched carefully) and mimicked. What a well-known CEO or senior leader does will be replicated by others aiming to have their level of success. Now, do we want that replication to be inclusive or exclusive?

I sat down with Anne Boden MBE to discuss demanding more from people like her in senior leadership positions and incorporating inclusion into Starling Bank from the beginning. Anne is a Welsh tech entrepreneur and the founder and CEO of Starling Bank, a UK digital bank. To say Anne is renowned in her field would be an understatement. She has held positions like Head of EMEA at RBS and COO at Allied Irish Bank, and now as CEO of Starling Bank, she has raised US $468 million in funding. This is impressive in itself, and even more so when you note that she is a woman in an extremely male-dominated industry.

To start the conversation, I asked Anne about her growth into leadership and how she has thrown herself into these kinds of roles. Doing anything different brings friction and sometimes naysayers – disrupting the banking industry is absolutely one of those things, where Anne herself has said 'banking was trying to pretend technology hadn't happened'. She said:

> If everything goes perfectly in your role, you never break new ground. If you go from one job to another, it's just an upwards trajectory, but you never challenge yourself. And in my career, I've been in lots of different places, with lots of sideways moves with many things I didn't expect to happen. With Starling Bank, this was something I had to do. I'd gone into Allied Irish Bank in 2012 and the role was very hard work, with lots of time spent slashing costs and, ultimately, causing people to be unhappy. I kept hearing this same story from different places around the world and one morning, I got up and decided that somebody should start a new bank. Now, I didn't think that could be me.

> I have spent my whole life in banking – I knew how it worked and I still felt quite disillusioned by it, because of the obstacles that existed. So when I quit my job to start a new bank, people were quite surprised. I clearly remember going to a networking event organized by upmarket exec coaches for people who leave their roles in C-suite positions. There were over 200 people from the top echelons of UK corporate life. I've been

in leadership positions for most of my life and I know that
role well. I'd just left my role at AIB and people were asking
me what I was doing next. I told them I was starting a bank.
They then asked who got me the job. I told them they didn't
understand and that I'm starting a bank and raising money.
They then would ask about co-founders and I replied that no, it
was just me. I even had a situation where one person said that
they would expect this other well-known middle-aged white
banking leader, who was a man, to start their own bank – but
not me.

So, despite being a senior leader in banking for most of my
life, I was already facing bias before I started because people
who start banks are middle-aged white men. They are not
five-foot-tall women from Wales. I've always done things that
people didn't expect me to do. My father left school at 14,
my mother left school at 15 and my father worked in the steel
works. I went to a large comprehensive school in the middle
of a huge council estate and we lived in a few old private
houses on the outskirts. Hardly anyone went to university. But
I had a lovely supportive father who believed that I could do
absolutely anything. So I went to Swansea University and when
I graduated, I had a job in Lloyds Bank and then I came up to
London to find a place to live. And all of us came – my mother,
my father and me – all in our touring caravan. This was a big
deal for us.

I started as a computer scientist in 1981 – there were two
women in the graduate intake and hardly any people that were
not privately educated. Throughout my career, I've always
been told that I'm extremely high performing and extremely
hard working, but probably have 'limited potential' to go to
the next stage. But I didn't accept that and each role I had, I
kept jumping over those people, I kept on working, breaking
boundaries and that's why I've been in leadership roles for most
of my life.

Anne's career is undoubtedly impressive. But it is clear that her role in leadership and into leadership has not been as smooth as it was for others. Before asking her about her suggestions on how we must demand more from people like her, I asked her about her experiences as a senior woman in banking:

> When you've been the only woman in the room, it means that there's no scope for failure.

> It means everybody notices and people think that you contribute more than you actually do. People distort your contribution in their mind. If they like you, they positively see their contribution. If they don't like you, then they see it negatively.

> With gender stereotypes at play, women spend a lot of time trying to make sure everybody in the room is comfortable. Right? We look after all the housekeeping and introduction chit-chat, then men come in, sit down and speak more than anyone else. We feel obliged to do all of that because we're uncomfortable in ourselves. And all these things added together mean that it is harder for us to get promotion. Right. It is harder for us to meet the expected standards for us. I can't know what this is like for women of colour because I don't know what it feels like not to be white. But I can imagine it is tough.

> I do know what it feels like to be the only woman, and the only person who didn't go to a public school. It took me a long time to understand that those differences weren't my fault. I spent a huge amount of my spare time reading absolutely every book I could on gender equality. By having this knowledge, it means I can make a stand and push the way for future leaders.

As a senior leader, not just in Starling but in her industry, Anne very clearly has an ability to influence the wider industry – and she does. I asked her about her view on the responsibility to leave things better than she got them and how Starling has embedded inclusion into their DNA and leadership:

> We have done lots of different initiatives to embed inclusion in our DNA. For example, we filter job ads to ensure the language is not biased towards certain groups.

> We held employees' forums in response to BLM, having started conversations at exec level. This work is focusing on role models and looking at the systems and how they work for everyone.

> We have launched an ongoing initiative called Never Home Alone since the introduction of remote working. This keeps employees in touch and on point. It aims to support wellbeing and good mental and physical health.

> I host 'Ask Anne' three times a week; it's a live-streamed event where we hold a 15 minute mini 'town hall' meeting at where I (or another colleague) answer staff questions live. It's open to everybody and they can ask anything.

> Externally, we liaise with outside groups to ensure our products and services are inclusive, for example for our gambling block we coordinate with gambling addiction and mental health organizations, we workshopped with the RNIB on design and we liaised with the Royal Voluntary Service, which recommended our Connected card for NHS volunteers.

> The Connected card itself is another example. It was launched just after lockdown started to ensure that people who are sheltering had a safe way to pay for groceries bought for them by friends and family.

> We do a lot of work both internally and externally, but by doing this we've been able to embed inclusion by default on our journey.

Anne has a wealth of experience, knowledge and insights in holding leadership roles in an array of banks. I asked her what her top suggestions are for people in positions like her to be more inclusive in their leadership:

> Firstly, be curious. Actually read, listen and participate. You need to break out of your own conceptual view of the world and challenge yourself with different readings and hearing different perspectives. It's great and exciting to stretch yourself.

> Secondly, embrace the change. The world now is getting more exciting, more challenging and hopefully getting fairer. Look forward to that even if it means some discomfort for yourself.

> Thirdly, listen to what your people want and need. Right now, we're seeing the mobilization of the Black Lives Matter movement in the middle of a global pandemic. You must listen to your people and hear them – really hear them. And use your leadership to support, advocate and make the world better for them.

> Fourthly, be aware of the biases in the world. Your own and those around you. I face a lot of gender and age bias, but there are many more at play. Remember that everyone comes from a different place. Notably, startup founders are typically guys in their 20s, who are willing to take a huge risk. Because they often have a safety net beneath them. That doesn't mean those that don't have that don't want to be or can't still be successful.

> Lastly, always set context. I spend a lot of time setting context at Starling with my team because that means we're all on the same page and can move fast. We never do internal presentations to each other. We say what we're going to do, point in the direction we're going and go – it's highly aligned, and loosely coupled. This means people can work in the best ways for them whilst still making an impact across the same goals.

It is incredibly clear that from Anne's direction and perspectives, Starling has taken a specific approach to reworking the banking industry. As the CEO, she has the privilege of deciding how, what and why the company does what it does.

For successful DE&I strategies to truly take roots, senior leadership must be willing to undertake a number of processes. We discuss a number of these next.

Challenge your peers

Being in an executive role means being surrounded by executives. Being in a powerful role usually means you are surrounded by other powerful people. Even if a company claims to be 'flat' or non-hierarchical, these roles will exist because, well, they need to for the company to exist and to get anything done. From the stats we've talked about before, it's clear that the majority of people in senior leadership positions are white, heterosexual, non-disabled men. Now, if those people have not gone on the journey to understand their privilege, bias and educate themselves on what that means in their way of working, then this means the few that have done this work will need to challenge them. Challenging peers and challenging those around you is not easy – it involves being willing to put yourself in a potential firing line, being the one that others do not agree with. We talked about 'performative allyship' earlier – if you are in one of these positions and you decide to stay quiet instead of using your voice to speak up, you are being performative.

Challenging your peers should always be done respectfully. We can be firm and clear, making our point heard. There will be times where you might want your leaders to not hire their friend from their past role, and spend the time widening the pipeline to find a more diverse pool to choose from, or when you should speak up because you have noticed micro-aggressions within the executive group and because they do not affect anyone within the group, they are allowed to slide. Leaders have to make the conscious decision to do more of this, do it more regularly and do it better.

Educate your teams

It's all well and good to challenge people, but you must provide education (or education opportunities) to these people too. People listen to leaders and what they say matters. Everyone is on a growth journey here (myself included) and if you have found things that have helped you widen your knowledge and mindset around privilege, bias, etc, then share these things. This is useful too when challenging people as it becomes a productive conversation. Instead of just telling people what not to do, telling them what not to do and providing them with education to learn is better. This is emotionally taxing work, but in leadership this is a responsibility. Please do also ensure this emotional tax is fairly split. Like I said, the majority of leaders are from a homogeneous group – make sure the only leader challenging and educating other leaders isn't the only one who doesn't identify with the majority.

I suggest leaders regularly call out the pieces they have found useful in their communications. Are you speaking at a company-wide event or sharing your newsletter? Drop in a note on the readings, articles, podcasts or people you're following online that have helped you in this space and why – role model the behaviour you want others in your organization to do (especially middle management – more on them soon).

Push against the systems that may have directly advantaged you

Becoming a leader is hard – it takes a lot of experience and education. I don't view leadership as needing a specific set of time to warrant the title, but I do view leadership as something granted to those who have earned it. There are people who are only a few years into their career and are leaders, and there are people who are many years into their career and aren't/don't want to be leaders. Either way, when you're in this position, it's important to think about how you got there and why.

No one is disputing that you have worked hard and that things may have been tough for you at some stage. What I am saying is that it is easier for some than others (remember the Privilege Walk exercise we did together). Now, this privilege and ease don't manifest themselves only hypothetically – they are in our processes like hiring, promotion, probation passing, palatability to others and more. When you're in the position of leadership, please remember to not climb the ladder and then pull it up afterwards. Just because things have been difficult for you doesn't mean we should enforce them being difficult for future and new leaders. That is immature, childish and, frankly, not leadership material. If you see your peers doing this, please reread 'Challenge your peers' (and challenge it!).

We must spend the time understanding how things may have worked in our favour, then actively push against these processes, raising the issues we may now be aware of, hiring the right people to analyse the data and amend them. Being silent is being willing to continue the system of disadvantage.

Allocate a budget to DE&I

This is self-explanatory. Leaders control budgets. Budgets are allocated to everything – product changes, hiring, promotions, company events and… DE&I. This means:

- Investing in a senior-level DE&I leader to help bring to light and life DE&I work in your organization (if you're not at the stage to hire like this, hire a short-term contractor to analyse and unearth were you're at, then assign someone to this *after* they have gone through appropriate training to warrant being in any DE&I junior manager role etc).

- Allocating budget for partnerships to empower and support current employees from various groups and aiming to widen your talent pipeline by reaching different people from under-represented demographics. This costs money as organizations dedicated to this space rightfully charge for conference slots, partnerships, job boards, etc. Choose organizations that align with your strategy, the demographics of people you're trying to reach and the areas you're trying to hire into.
- Allocating budget for employee resource groups, which are groups (more on how to set them up for success later) that need money to run events and socials throughout the year. This can be done relatively cheaply; however, for flagship events such as Black History Month, Pride, International Women's Day, etc a larger budget will be required. Budget also comes in the form of employee time and the people running these groups should be given appropriate funded time to do so.

Make unbiased decisions

Going on this journey is tough and making unbiased decisions is no mean feat. It takes time, education, self-awareness and an ability to comfortably admit when you're wrong (something many lack). Before making a decision, allocate time to thinking about who the decision affects, what the effect will be for differ-ent people and why that is – then think about how you get the best outcome for everyone. There will be times where you have to make difficult decisions and that is expected. However you must be confident these are unbiased and are able to still deliver the difficult message empathetically. At every stage of the process, there should be appropriate checks to ask the following questions:

- How have we actively ensured this will work for marginalized communities?

- Have we gathered enough requirements from different user personas to understand if this covers all appropriate bases?
- Do we have any user research to back up our view that this is inclusive and anti-racist? If so, what are the findings?
- Have we tested this thoroughly with a diverse data set?
- Do we know without doubt that this change/application/new service etc will not cause harm to a specific group of people?

Leaders have the ability to shape the entire company culture because they are the pinnacle of what is expected – they are the role models. However, they are not always the people with direct contact to those from underrepresented groups. That's middle management.

The role of middle management in successful DE&I strategies

Underrepresented people are more greatly represented in junior and mid-tier positions, meaning they are not directly liaising with senior management in their day-to-day work. They are directly working with middle management. Middle management is the managers who sit between senior leadership and the rest of the business, taking the vision and strategy into the organization and managing it from an operational point of view. Their role isn't entirely to develop the vision, they feed into it and bring it to life with the help of the people they lead.

Middle managers are notoriously hard to engage in DE&I work because their focus is heavily on getting things done now and execution – anything meaning they need to slow down isn't always viewed positively. Senior leadership are focused on long-term strategy. Because of this very clear focus on day-to-day delivery, it can be difficult to firstly engage middle management and, secondly, for them to be able to really lean into making this work part of their ways of working. So, why should these people have a role in the success of DE&I strategies?

Firstly, these people bring to life the senior management and company vision. If they are not aligned with what senior leadership is trying to achieve, then it will not come to fruition. What will happen in this case is disconnection between words and action, and this will be directly damaging to the DE&I efforts. Senior management may define the vision of the organization, but these people are the ones who bring it to life and embed it down into the company.

Secondly, these people are in direct contact with those who are more likely to be in lower/middle roles and who will benefit from these DE&I efforts. They need to understand why this work is being done and what their role is because, otherwise, the people who really need their managers to be on board and engaged won't be – and they will feel let down and potentially continue to struggle with processes that were not made with them in mind.

For successful DE&I strategies to truly take roots, a good DE&I strategy should engage middle management in a number of ways. Let's look at this in more depth.

Embedding inclusive behaviours into performance reviews

DE&I makes good business sense (we've talked about this in detail throughout this book), but for people to really understand that it must be part of the company's DNA; it must be integrated into your performance reviews. Performance reviews happen typically annually and consist of 'a formal assessment in which managers evaluate an employee's work performance, identify strengths and weaknesses, offer feedback, and set goals for future performance' (BambooHR, 2019). Their role is to understand how an employee is currently working, with conversations tying promotion to benefits or salary increases. They play a key role in any employee's experience and they play an even bigger role in the success of DE&I strategies.

Middle management has the potential to be the future senior management of tomorrow. With this in mind, inclusive leadership behaviours must be part of the criteria they are assessed against to make sure they are bringing to life any inclusion strategy. This will mean they will need to demonstrate alignment and engagement with inclusion-related initiatives such as sponsoring more junior/mid-tier people from underrepresented groups, actively championing inclusion through sharing learnings on diversity with their peer group, ensuring diverse shortlists for the areas they are hiring on and allocating budget towards partnerships/events for their teams to attend to empower different marginalized groups.

Leadership values (which should be inclusive) must be incorporated into how you evaluate people, otherwise they are simply words on a page. And by directly linking inclusive leadership to promotions, therefore linking it to pay, you can engage a group of people who may be more resistant.

For example, think about how 'growing the business' value may translate into inclusion. This could be viewed as simply expanding, hiring and increasing revenue. But it should also be translated into understanding how to grow employees from different backgrounds, helping them reach their full potential, whatever that might be. To evaluate whether a manager is doing this, 360 feedback should be gathered from their teams to see whether they are really bringing to life the culture vision that senior management is describing.

Directly involving them in what you're trying to achieve

Like I said before, middle managers are the people who bring to life the corporate vision. This means that in their remits, they will (hopefully) be respected and looked to for guidance, advice and even pastoral care. They have the avenues to be able to directly push down communications, initiatives and successes/ growth areas in the DE&I strategy. Not all communications need to come from your DE&I director. Utilize the channels that work best to both deliver an authentic message and engage those that are crucial to your success. This also gives you an opportunity to have middle-management review communications (when relevant) so they land in the best way for their people – they will obviously know them best.

Your DE&I committee should have representation from middle management to ensure you're truly understanding the problems you're trying to solve. A senior view can sometimes cloud the day-to-day issues because they're not 'down in the weeds'. Never make an assumption on what people need. Instead, ask them.

Linking DE&I to business growth and goals

Ideally, everyone would understand why DE&I work is important because it is the right thing to do and, simply, we should all be uncomfortable and unwilling to accept an entirely unjust society. However, that is not how the world works. We must accept that many people are driven more by business needs and therefore tap into this to drive a meaningful impact.

DE&I strategies may focus on the 'right thing to do' point, but they should also focus on how this drives business growth and demand. Businesses prioritizing DE&I have healthier bottom lines, have an ability to reach top-tier talent that simply demands to work for an organization that prioritizes having this work, and have the potential to widen their customer base purely because the services will resonate with more audiences.

There is a very real need to reach and widen talent pools and DE&I strategies aim to do just that. Middle management plays an important role in all of this work, but their engagement will be entirely dependent on how senior management discusses these topics and allocates appropriate resources to make it happen. For example, if they expect middle managers to widen their talent pipeline and have diverse shortlists yet still make a hire in the same timeframe that was expected before this extra work was required, then it simply won't happen. There has to be an understanding of scales of balance on both sides.

Scaling inclusion efforts as you grow

DE&I work is not the same at a company of 100 people vs that of 10,000 and above. The notable differences tend to come when you break the 300–400 person mark, the 1,000 mark, the 5,000 mark and then the 10,000 mark and upwards. This usually means you're across different regions, have employees of varying tenures and have people outside of the initial echo chamber you may have hired for. There is a lot to take on board and into account when developing any DE&I strategy. Building a strategy that scales is crucial.

Your workplace will shift and move as much as society does and you should be able to flex your strategy easily to meet these growing demands. This means having a really strong structure in place – strong foundations allow for unexpected needs and changes; just think about how much shifting DE&I leaders had to do in 2020 with the impact of the global Covid-19 pandemic and the mobilization of Black Lives Matter movements globally.

It's important to align your mission to now *and* the future, not just now. This will enable people to easily get behind this work, even if the focus shifts slightly and requires a new way of engagement. Entirely changing missions usually means due diligence hasn't been done up front, therefore DE&I 'leaders' (or those in these roles with little experience other than lived perspectives) and business leaders have to scramble to rework focus and goals to engage and widen their work in a rush.

We'll now look at how to scale effectively.

Invest in a system that measures eNPS and belonging

Employee Net Promoter Score (eNPS) is a concept that builds off the NPS system, allowing employers to measure and get a snapshot of employees' willingness to be ambassadors for the company by advocating employment there. The NPS, which the employee version is based on, is a concept pioneered and trademarked by Bain & Company, Satmetrix Systems, Inc. and Fred Reichheld. It was designed as a way to measure customer loyalty by organizing customers into promoters, passives and detractors with the question 'how likely are you to recommend this company to a friend or relative?' (CultureIQ, 2015). Promoters (those that answered 9–10) are the most loyal segment who will enthusiastically recommend employment at a company. Passives (those that answered 6–8) are those that are not necessarily negative but are also not entirely loyal. Detractors (those that answered 0–5) are those that are not likely to recommend employment at the company and it's important to get to the bottom of why that is. Utilizing this methodology, with questions that directly ask about DE&I and non-discrimination allow you to have a continuous temperature check on where you're at, what's working and what isn't.

There are lots of great tools out there to do this and ones like Peakon, which offer monthly cadence of surveys, with customizable questions, useful learning resources tied to certain drivers, an ability to capture employee attribute data safely (more on why this is important in a moment) and a heatmap breakdown of what's going well and what isn't.

The key piece here is being able to capture employee attribute data safely as part of the survey, meaning you get a much clearer picture of what inclusion and belonging actually mean to your base. Otherwise, you get a blanket view of (for example) 80 per cent of people enjoy working at company X; however, if your employee base is predominately white, heterosexual, non-disabled men, then are you really getting a true picture to understand how people who don't identify with this group feel?

Set your goals

What are you trying to achieve and why? What are you basing these goals on – perspectives, data, employee insights, societal intervention, or a mix of all of these? Decide what you want to achieve both from a 'vision' perspective and a metric perspective. Metrics don't only have to be focused on representation percentages; they can also be focused on eNPS scores to measure inclusion, belonging, non-discrimination, etc.

You should define quarterly milestones that are reported to the C-suite and board, ensuring accountability and clear initiatives that bolster the metrics you're discussing.

Understand the regions where your business is based

Census data and employee HQs are super important to understand. There is a difference in what a DE&I strategy looks like in Copenhagen rather than in London, or London rather than in Dhaka, or London rather than in Edinburgh, and so on. Cities have different representations (especially from an ethnicity perspective), alongside different cultural influences that have changed and formed the ways of working in those areas. For example, consider countries where religion is deeply embedded, such as Italy or Saudi Arabia and remember how this will feed into gender stereotypes and, therefore, different barriers for women that don't exist to the same extent in other countries. Or the representation of people of colour in places like Ireland or Switzerland etc. This is not making excuses for why you may lack diversity in those spaces, but it's important to paint this as a whole, clear picture. It is unrealistic to compare a company with a base in London (where 40 per cent of the population is from Black, Asian or minority ethnic backgrounds) to a company with a base in Northern Ireland (where 2 per cent of these same communities are represented). Spend the time understanding this data and where your business may scale to.

Embed data collection early

Data is incredibly important in DE&I, yet so many organizations have not prioritized this and are scrambling to put together half-hearted strategies focusing on community and employee resource groups only. Embed this early through a strong HR information system that allows you to capture employee characteristic data across gender identity, ethnicity, disability, neurodiversity, caring responsibilities, religion, sexual orientation, transgender identification and economic background. What's important here is that you have a very succinct and clean-cut communications plan as to why you're asking employees to share this sensitive information with you, how you will safeguard it, who has access and what you plan to do with it. You'll only ever be reporting on aggregate and it should be locked down to a very select few people. Every field should have a Prefer Not To Say option so people can opt in with what they're comfortable with and opt out of what they're not.

We spoke about intersectionality in depth earlier. Having this array of data allows you to have an intersectional approach, ensuring you get a full picture of representation and what is happening in terms of retention, attrition, leavers, etc.

Engage leadership

This might sound like a no-brainer but engaging leadership early and regularly allows scaling. It's imperative you bring the decision makers along in this journey, even if that means conversations that challenge and push against this. Spend time embedding this type of relationship early so when things get busy (they will) and time is stretched, this is still part of their role and business decision-making process. Understand business growth goals and how your DE&I strategy bolsters them.

Engaging is more than just words. Accountability is also key – ensure in your strategy there is ownership of metrics (whether this is eNPS or employee representation, hiring, etc) with those that sit in the business – think engineering, product, design leadership, etc. Make sure this is baked into how they are reviewed in salary conversations and performance reviews. That means they *have* to be engaged as this is part of their role and another area they're directly measured on.

You will need to ask for a lot of changes, budget and process rework with DE&I. There will be times where the answer is 'no' to what you ask and you also have to be prepared for what you will do then. There will be many occasions where continuously pushing makes sense, and times when it doesn't. During Covid-19, many organizations made their Heads of DE&I redundant or fired them to scale back costs, only to then try to hire them back after the social unrest in relation to the treatment of Black employees (Anderson, 2020). Think smart, be forceful and be clear on what you want. Do not shy away from pushing people hard and calling people out who are directly perpetuating the things you're trying to fix. You will have to be comfortable in doing this otherwise, you are spending more time on words than action. If you can't do this, get someone into the role who can.

Demanding more is never easy, but it is necessary. And to do so, we must engage different parts of the business in different ways that align with how they operate and work.

References

Anderson, B (2020) [accessed 13 December 2020] Why the Head of Diversity is the Job of the Moment [Online] https://business.linkedin.com/talent-solutions/blog/diversity/2020/why-the-head-of-diversity-is-the-job-of-the-moment (archived at https://perma.cc/AFD5-AZ2X)

BambooHR (2019) [accessed 13 December 2020] What is a Performance Review? [Online] www.bamboohr.com/hr-glossary/performance-review/ (archived at https://perma.cc/ZSV9-TC4N)

CultureIQ (2015) [accessed 13 December 2020] The Employee Net Promoter Score: The What, the Why, the How [Online] https://cultureiq.com/blog/employee-net-promoter-score (archived at https://perma.cc/N5YQ-83JK)

CHAPTER EIGHT

Planning for more

This chapter will focus on:

- Moving past 'being nice'
- The different uses of quotas
- Data, data and more data
- Creating communities
- Moving forward

We've discussed privilege, bias, intersectionality, allyship and more. With this knowledge, awareness and understanding, we must prepare, strategize and move forward with purpose. I've made it clear that equity does not just happen, in the same way that inequity does not just happen – each of these things is measured, deliberate and purposeful. To combat inequity and unfairness, we must plan for more – and plan well.

Moving past 'being nice'

We've touched on this before, but I want us to think about how many people view 'being nice' as a benchmark for inclusion.

'Being nice' is a quantifier we use for whether we like people or not. Likeability is a very real factor in how we decide if we want to work with someone – if we can see ourselves getting on really well with them. It's also used as a quantifier as a way to disregard underrepresented people's experiences because someone is 'too nice' to have done something shocking, bad or inappropriate.

How often have you heard 'oh, that can't be true. They are so nice. You must be overreacting or taking it the wrong way'. How often have you said that yourself (or thought it)? When we view niceness as the barrier to belief, we underestimate the insidious nature of exclusion, sexism, racism, homophobia, ableism and so on. Niceness is also entirely subjective. What you view as nice, someone else might not, which obviously means this is rife for bias and biased-driven actions.

But how does 'niceness' or lack thereof affect inclusion? 'Niceness' is riddled with bias. It's also used to augment how tragic something is. 'Oh that was such a tragedy, they were a pillar of society', 'Oh, I can't believe that happened to them. They were the nicest person'. Now, whilst you may not believe something could possibly have happened at the hands of someone you like, that doesn't mean your view of them absolves them of any potential wrongdoing. I also want us to think about using this as a quantifier for caring. For example, when Jonathan Price was murdered at the hands of police (Shaun Lucas has been charged with the murder of Jonathan), Twitter was flooded with comments around how Jonathan was an upstanding member of society and community – a 'Hometown Hero' (Midkiff, 2020). All of these things can be true, but would this murder have been viewed as less tragic if Jonathan were not a 'Hometown Hero', but rather just a regular man. It's important that whilst we might understand why the media paints stories in this way, it can potentially mean we view other stories or deaths as less impactful or important.

The different uses of quotas

A quota is setting a limit or target on the number of people or things that are officially allowed or given entry. Ordinarily, when people hear the word 'quota' in terms of DE&I strategies, they shudder or immediately disengage, but hear me out. Quotas can be a significant gear-shifter in the world of diversity because it forces us to look at our processes and mindsets. It's very easy to say something is inclusive just because you *think* it is, but if you set a certain quota and never meet it, then it's clear your beliefs are wrong.

Many organizations and countries have utilized quotas to effect real change. Across the world, different governments for countries and regions have enforced different gender diversity quotas on corporate boards. For example, in India, the Companies Act 2013 imposes a quota of at least one female director on the board of listed companies and any public company having a paid-up share capital of 100 crore or more rupees or a turnover of 300 crore or more rupees (Terjesen, Aguilera and Lorenz, 2014). In 2006, Norway introduced quota legislation that required both public and state-owned companies to have 40 per cent female board representation by 2008. Failure to comply resulted in fines or company closures. Full compliance was achieved by 2009. The percentage of female board members has since remained between 36 and 40 per cent (Gov.UK, 2011). Many other countries or regions such as Pakistan, the Middle East, North America and Australia have followed suit. Unfortunately, in the UK, the government has opted for advice vs quotas, which has meant a less consistent, opt-in approach. Those who care will do it voluntarily; those who don't will not and be happy to avoid accountability.

As we've seen throughout this book, diverse boards create better companies. Despite these clear wins, these quotas are not without controversy – as you'd expect. Some might view these as forcing something where it doesn't fit and giving jobs based on gender vs skillset. However, I'd urge you to consider that without clear, strategic and measurable initiatives (like these), we cannot realistically and efficiently undo the years and years of exclusion that have created the society, boards and companies we're now dealing with.

Another good example of this is the Rooney Rule, which we chatted about earlier in Chapter 5 'Check yourself: Unchecked and unconscious biases' and utilizing ways to disrupt them in hiring. 'Originally implemented by the National Football League (NFL) and named after Pittsburgh Steelers chairman Dan Rooney, the original Rooney Rule sought to increase the opportunities for minorities to hold NFL head coaching positions. The results were impressive – minority head coaching hires in the NFL increased from 6% to 22% in 2006' (Cook, 2015). This is about forcing us to find talent in the pools we're simply ignoring right now. And it doesn't have to be used for boards only. Many organizations use these kinds of metrics and quotas to help ensure diverse representation throughout their organization, such as Pinterest where they aim to fill 30 per cent of full-time engineering roles with women and 8 per cent with people of underrepresented ethnic backgrounds (Lorenzetti, 2015).

I want you to think of quotas as enabling everyone (and I mean everyone) to compete for the jobs they want – right now, many do not have the opportunity to compete, despite being qualified (sometimes more than). What we want to do is give everyone the fair opportunity to compete – and know that if they're the best person for the job, they'll get it. Please keep in mind there is a lot of work to do to be able to comfortably say that we're giving a 'fair opportunity' and that our process isn't riddled with bias.

It's also important to remember that diversity numbers are only one side of this equation. It's all well and good having a diverse board on the surface, but what about the real inclusion of these people? We can bring all of the different perspectives and voices into a room, but if they are not actually heard then what's the point? We've spoken already about really listening to someone vs waiting for your turn to speak. Remember that diversity without inclusion is fruitless.

Data, data and more data

You've come this far into this book and, by now, you'll know how important data is to me – and how important it should be to you too. Without data, we are making huge, sweeping assumptions and regularly swapping individual and personal experience for fact-based insights. Both should work hand in hand, but never one without the other.

Assumptions are riddled with bias and personal experience is just that – personal. Now groups of people may have collective similar experiences and these are all entirely valid. What is important is that you back up these experiences with data, therefore allowing you to track if things get better, worse or stay the same.

For example, let's say Black people in a team share that they feel like they've been discriminated against more than their white counterparts. What do you do next? Firstly, let's gather data (ideally using an intelligent employee experience platform if you can afford one; using a Google form will work for a short period of time, but it doesn't scale as it only provides a one-off insight) that allows you to see if there is a trend in this thought process across the company. Then let's analyse your grievance process to see 1) if it's fit for purpose to actually be used by Black people and people of colour (are your HR staff trained appropriately, especially if they are non-Black, to deal with ethnicity-related issues?), 2) if it's being used right now by Black people at all and 3) what the rates are of actionable outcomes for ethnicity-related grievances (and any grievance raised by a Black person) vs all other grievances. Then, you need to look at the overall ratings given in performance reviews by middle management to Black people – is there bias in there? Are they being treated harsher than their white counterparts? What have you done to counteract that?

Without having data rooted at your core and throughout your company's DNA, you can't answer any of the questions above. Many of you may be at the start of this journey, and that is ok. What I suggest is that you:

1 *Understand what data you're capturing at the moment and where. What HR Information System (HRIS) are you using?* Is it fit for purpose, ie does it allow you to add custom fields? Are the fields currently provided inclusive (ie gender fields not limited to male/female)? Can it connect to an employee experience platform so you can measure inclusion as well as diversity? What reporting does it offer?

2 *Discuss why the data you're capturing already is being captured.* It is likely you are only capturing gender because of mandatory needs for pension setup and so on, but it's important to understand if conversations have been had to widen this capture in the past and if that hasn't been successful, why not?

3 *Understand your organization by localization and/or region.* Link in with your legal team (never just capture this data without legal approval – I've been in places that have done this and the cleanup is not good). There are restrictions in certain countries around capturing ethnicity-related data, for example. It's also important to understand the local terms and categories for ethnicity, disability and so on. There isn't a one-size-fits-all approach here, so spend the time analysing what you need, what regions you need, what the government/ credible organization suggestions are and then run all thoughts through your legal team. They must approve everything.

4 *Be realistic.* Now, whilst I always suggest capturing data across gender identity, ethnicity, sexual orientation, age (you can get this from your HRIS anyway), neurodiversity, disability, caring

responsibilities and mental health, not everyone is in a position to start there. At a minimum, capture gender identity and ethnicity to allow for an overlap and intersectional approach to capture the impact on different people from different ethnic groups. This is a starting point and you should communicate that as such.

5   *Communicate and communicate regularly.*

You'll want to get a decent disclosure rate (75–80 per cent in your company is good) to allow you to spot meaningful trends and themes, and enable the creation of quotas (for gender and ethnicity (based on census data), for example). People won't always share this data readily (depending on how data-driven your company already is), so it's important you:

a. State where you are right now – clearly communicate what stage you're at, ie report the data you already have or share that you don't have any and that this is now a priority for you to remedy.

b. Inform why you're asking for this data – what's the strategy? What are you aiming to do with the data? Will you use it to judge if processes are fair and unbiased and also ensure you are regularly on top of where your employee breakdowns are?

c. Share what you'll do with it – will you form quotas? Will it form the basis of external commitments for you? Will you sign up to some charters that aim to help you increase your underrepresented numbers?

d. Regularly update – how often will you report to the board/ C-suite on it? Will you share those updates company-wide too (I suggest you do)? To aid a consistent and good disclosure rate, share this (alongside the data analysis) each quarter broken down by business area/team, depending on your organization size. Then tie the responsibility for increasing this to business leaders to each of those remits to ensure the onus of DE&I data is not solely on one single person. Their responsibility to report will be one person's (or a team's) but it isn't just their job to take the organization on this journey. It's also likely when you break down this data by business unit level, some healthy competition will form and you can use that to spur on completion. Remember, this is optional data so it's unlikely you'll ever reach 100 per cent – but we can try!

6 *Embed data collection into your onboarding process.*
   This is common sense but without doing this, you will always be fighting a fire of an ever-decreasing disclosure rate.

The best advice I can give you is to intertwine your DE&I data into absolutely everything – do not make decisions without it or without considering the positive, negative or indifferent effect those decisions will have on it. It's time to get serious about inclusion. And to get serious, we must treat this like part of the business, in the same way we treat our engineering, operations, sales, product, design, marketing, etc decisions.

Creating communities

Community is important. People coming together is always part of inclusion. But what is important is that you elevate it to be more than just coming together.

Do you have employee resource groups? We've spoken about these before (and Kike shared some great tips on how to make them successful). If you have them, do they have a consistent framework, budget and lines of communication with your DE&I leader/s and other senior leadership? These communities must also have their leads funded. Depending on your business size, that might mean they are quite literally paid for their time in running them in the form of giving them a number of allocated days as part of their job to run the group and that their activities (and success or failure of these activities) form part of their progression conversations, alongside their technical delivery of their day job.

I also suggest that you utilize the voices in these groups (and others) to form a Think Tank or council that should meet every one to two months to share their thoughts, perspectives, insights and experiences of the current DE&I strategy you have in place. I see this as a way to put many different lenses on the one solution/strategy. This avoids creating an echo chamber or a siloed view of how this work is going. It also creates another connection for junior/mid-tier employees to senior leadership.

Moving forward

We all want to move forward – we don't want to go backwards and we know that isn't an acceptable movement. To discuss how to move forward, with scale in mind, I chatted to Brian Reaves, the Chief Diversity and Inclusion Officer at Dell. Brian is responsible for Dell's global diversity and inclusion initiatives. In his role, he partners with leaders and team members across the organization to deepen and advance Dell's culture of inclusion as a fundamental business imperative. His experience is impressive – as you'd expect. His background is in software engineering (like me!) and over the past 30 years, Brian has held senior executive software development and management roles in a number of industries/technology sectors including cloud computing, supply chain, healthcare, finance, telecommunications and utilities. He has witnessed first-hand many of the problems we are all trying to solve and fix.

Given this extensive background and experience, it only made sense to ask Brian how he had seen the industry shift towards DE&I. Has it been mostly positive or negative? He said:

> I think overall the net has been mostly positive. The more change happens, the more those who don't like change will push back.
>
> We have definitely evolved over the years from things like affirmative action, where specific steps have been implemented

to increase the representation of typically underrepresented people. A lot of people saw them as mandates. And people don't like being told to do something, especially if it's not something they truly believe in themselves or understand. But the difference between those days and now is in three dimensions:

1 Unlike back then, people have proof with regards to the correlation of diversity, inclusion and equity, to business outcomes. It's gone from 'this is a nice thing to do' to now having people pay attention. Greater innovation, greater employee engagement, greater employee retention – all those things net out to a creative top line or bottom line.

2 The second thing that has changed is global purchasing power. Everybody knows that the world's demographics are changing generationally, where you have 75 per cent of the workforce soon being a millennial or younger. Gender and ethnicity wise, both from representation, there's always for the most part been more women than men in the world. But from the purchasing power perspective of women and the intersection of ethnicity, global purchasing power is increasing exponentially. So, as a company, you pay attention and pattern yourselves to be able to track growth.

3 Everybody is struggling with the global talent shortage, most notably in tech. And there's no other way to solve it than by being more inclusive and going beyond where you traditionally recruit for talent.

Brian's work is clearly focused on supporting and ensuring people from different backgrounds can thrive, grow and succeed, meeting their goals, whatever they may be. This work is emotionally exhausting and it can take its toll – I can attest to that. Many people leading in this space are the kinds of people we are trying to make things better for. Brian is a Black American man and very obviously is affected by whether society is inclusive or not. Having spent so many years in engineering, I asked Brian what was the moment (or moments) that drove him to dedicate his career to DE&I leadership. Was it a specific moment when he pivoted into DE&I work from engineering… or simply a culmination of experiences that so many of us share? He said:

> I don't really view it as a pivot. As an engineer with degrees – in math or computer science – I always gravitated to try to solve complex business problems. And I did that with software back in the day – it was always about the business problem. It didn't matter what language I was using; I was trying to build software or lead teams who are building software to solve complex business problems.
>
> Now I have the same mindset, and it's an even more complex business problem. At least in software, you can write software and some things are predictable, but human beings are not. And that's what makes what you and I do so complex at times. Machines and large problems that have had some historical perspective to them are mostly predictable. But that's why I really believe the mindset that I bring to it is still that engineering mindset.
>
> My passion for this topic is really driven by how I was brought up. In South Central Los Angeles, where the vast majority of people – certainly Black men – did not have good life outcomes, you were either incarcerated or not on this earth by the time you were 21. The vast majority of my friends are no longer with us. This does not mean that they weren't smart and they couldn't do what I've done. It's just that they didn't have opportunity. The difference between me and my friends was that my family invested everything in me so that I didn't have that outcome. I had the opportunity to be educated. And then once I got that education, that changed everything for me and changed things for them as well.
>
> As I became an engineer, for all those years, creating opportunities was always top of mind for me – I remembered that was the difference. Opportunity changes everything. And that's what I view DE&I as – creating strategies and tactics so that everyone

can have an opportunity to succeed. And some may or may not choose to, but the fact that you are given opportunities means you can have the tools to change your life.

Brian's life experience undoubtedly has influenced his interest and dedication to this work. But I also wanted to know if there was a specific moment or time and place when he realized taking a technically minded approach (one that I very much align with also taking) to DE&I was something he should do full time, as opposed to doing it on top of his engineering leadership:

> So five years ago, when I was working at SAP, I was doing this work as a side hustle – doing different interesting things to enable opportunities for people at different places like HBCUs [Historically Black Colleges or Universities] and other underrepresented places.

> The CEO of SAP at the time convinced me that that same mindset should and could be applied more formally to DE&I because it was a different way than how SAP was focusing and thinking about it at the time. He convinced me to shift and that's what put me on Dell's radar. I view it just as another complex business problem bringing in different techniques to try to solve it. But I think, ultimately, if you, I and others are successful in this, it's going to open up opportunities for a lot of people, which, in essence, will make everybody and everything better in the world.

When we talk about 'opening up opportunities for a lot of people', global corporations and businesses have a responsibility to do this. These are the organizations that people listen to, pay attention to and likely use every single day probably without realizing. Dell is one of those organizations. One of the largest technology corporations in the world, it employs more than 165,000 people in the United States and around the world – making it one of the biggest PC companies globally. The responsibility is clearly there. I asked Brian how Dell is using this responsibility and power for good – both in their DE&I strategy and business mission. He said:

> We have the privilege to have the founder, chairman and CEO of this company to really get it. And that's Michael Dell. There are a lot of successful people in the world and you can put them in different categories. The most positive category you can put someone in who's had significant success is one where they recognize that success brings them the ability to do some significant, powerful things. Our mission is to drive human progress. For us, as a global organization, you're absolutely right – we have the ability to use this for good.
>
> Diversity and inclusion follow our mission closely. The things I get to do every day and even more broadly have a substantial social impact. We talked about those goals around sustainability, whether it's around ethics, privacy or improving the lives of a billion people by 2030, or in my remit, ensuring globally that women and, in the United States, Black, African American, Hispanic or Latino talents are represented. They all fit into this business narrative we were just speaking about earlier. Michael is very, very clear on what diversity and inclusion bring – and what equity brings is a company that is more like its customers who can serve them better. It can thrive and hence, given our mission, we can have others thrive.
>
> It is a privilege and an honour to actually represent this topic at a company where it is in the DNA and the person who founded the company supports you. What's important here is that Michael [Dell] will actively talk and bring up the topic of DE&I, regardless of what other issues he's talking about – because it's all linked.
>
> With regards to a number of initiatives that I feel have made a real notable impact:
>
> - *Training 165,000 Dell employees* – when I arrived three years ago, we had our 'Many advocating real change' programme

in place, which is our foundational learning around things like micro-aggression, privilege, unconscious bias, etc and the plan was to have our most senior leaders do this. When I looked at that platform, I said it's not about just our executives, it's about everybody. Back then, it was called 'Men advocating real change' – in my first week, I changed it to 'many', because it's not just about men, it's about all of us. But it was clear training leaders was not enough. I defined a goal that in a number of years we would have everyone at Dell gain this foundational learning. That meant moving our goal from hundreds of people to 165,000. But I wanted us to hold everybody accountable. That was a huge, huge win.

• *CEO commitment* – a more recent one around the time of George Floyd's death was reviewing our Culture Code. That details how we all work and it's led with inclusion of who we are. We lead with being inclusive people, as a community of team members, as leaders, and then adding all different questions to measure inclusivity, very, very prescriptively. It's one thing to say you want to be the employer of choice for all, it's another thing to tell the world what specifically that looks like, and have these audacious goals that shake everybody up, and you have to make progress. I think for a lot of our companies, the moment of truth is when something really bad happens. It's ok when good things are going well – people either opt in or out. After the death of George Floyd, our CEO wrote a letter to the whole company (Dell, 2020). He asked all of us to look at ourselves and consider what greater role we should play in moving the world forward. From that, I am leading an initiative called 'Standing strong together' focusing on moving our impact and support for Black team members faster than we even said before, based on having an empathetic view into what experience our Black team members are having. In that moment, and I told Michael [Dell] this, he moved the company because he is the founder. You can move the company whichever way because your name is on the building, and his response literally moved the company.

CEO commitment and senior leadership commitment are key here. We can't move the needle on inclusion without the buy-in from those who are the decision makers, the vision creators and the business drivers. However, they are not the only people that must be engaged. Middle management (which we've talked about in detail just before this chapter) must be engaged. Given the size of Dell's organization, middle management clearly plays an important role in the success of any initiative, no less DE&I. I asked Brian how he views the role of these people in any DE&I strategy and if he views them as crucial... or not. He said:

> I think they are fundamental. I'd be hard pressed to find
> an example of a company that doesn't have some sort of
> middle – and if you don't move that middle, you're not going
> to be successful, because they make the vast majority of hiring
> decisions, promotion decisions, attrition decisions and so on.
> With how the world works, the middle is what really dictates
> any movement, one way or another.

> In our line of work, there's this concept of the 'frozen middle'
> or the 'broken rung on the ladder', where a lot of companies
> focus initiatives to get more talent into the pipe at early talent
> levels. But that talent moving up the middle is determined by
> the current middle managers – they decide who gets to thrive
> or make their way into leadership because you don't externally
> hire most senior people. Getting this group the foundational
> learning, holding them accountable to the results such as
> diverse hiring shortlists and so on is key. That is the core of the
> strategy. So focusing top down. And then bottom up through
> our Employee Resource Groups. We have over 13 ERGs, with
> 50,000 unique people in one or more groups and they're the
> most passionate people. The strategy must nod to both, so
> we can influence top down and bottom up, but we absolutely
> have to get the middle to react to that influence. And if that
> happens, then you start to get that linearity of success across
> the board.

To engage all of these different types of people, managers and leaders, we must have a clear strategy. Getting linearity of success is no mean feat and it takes time. There is no 'silver bullet' for DE&I, but there are many ways to begin to do this work, building in scale, success measures, risk plans and more. Brian's work spans one of the world's largest global corporations – so who better to ask for top tips on how to help organizations plan for me – embedding DE&I into processes in a way that scales.

Brian's top tips are:

1 *Deeply understand the business imperative narrative* – when you approach to get those leaders on board, be clear on 'the why'. Get the narrative where you detail why we're talking about this, why our customers expect us to do it and that talent we're trying to attract expects us to have it. And in fact, if we're not successful in this area, there's some we're going to lose, both from a cultural and financial perspective.

2 *Drive for more transparency* – once you have the narrative, you must then understand where you sit today. You need to have more than HR or a small subset of people understand or see these numbers. If you want to get everyone on board, they need to at least know well how we measure our DE&I efforts, across what dimensions and then where we are today, because no company ever gets from point A to Z without having a goal of what they want Z to look like.

3 *Set broad goals and be accountable* – once you figure out where you are, then start whether it's smaller, more regular steps, or you go like we did (which is more typical of global, enterprise-sized businesses) and set audacious goals across a longer time period. Because certainly in Dell, and I would argue any company, if you can't measure it, it's not going to happen. But once you publicize and state those goals as widely as possible, you have accountability. Sometimes companies are a little frayed because it can bring external pressure to meet those goals that they don't want. But that's the point, right? If you want to put

the goals out there that you think you can feasibly reach, then you hold yourself and everybody accountable. And the best way to do that is by being transparent, both internally and externally. Tell the world 'Hey, we're not perfect. But here's the path we're going on and our aspirations'. And when we're not doing very well, we will tell you that, clearly explaining what's happened and how we're going to pivot – just like every other part of the business. Nobody's secret about their strategy, their innovation or whatever they're very boastful about. Yet, magically around this topic, many are substantially less transparent.

4 *Leaders to embrace vulnerability* – a lot of folks are scared to talk about politics or religion in companies. But guess what, you're going to be talking about a lot of both. Because that's what's on people's minds, alongside conversations on racism, sexism and so on. Now, great leaders listen. We went through our listening sessions after the death of George Floyd and our leaders sat and had to hear some tough things. And as a leader, because you're always in front, you usually have to have an answer. It is very vulnerable to not have an answer to something. With these topics, employees know that leaders may have many of the business answers, but for this, they need us to just listen right now and then work with them on education – coming up with an answer together.

I'd be lying if I said I wasn't a huge fan of Brian's and that everything he says resounds so clearly with me. I approach DE&I in the exact same way and it is a real privilege to hear his vision and see how he has brought it to life. His passion is clear but, more importantly, his delivery and skillset in this space are clearer. We've talked in detail about how to bring your business on this journey, embedding in inclusive processes, challenging those who don't get it and educating the masses, but I also wanted to talk to Brian about his personal experiences, especially as a Black man in the United States. We both share similar experiences of being underrepresented yet privileged. Now, as an Asian woman, I can never experience the same experiences Brian has (or a Black woman has), but there are similarities in some different ways. I asked Brian how he traverses that space as an Executive at one of the world's largest corporations whilst also being a Black man in a country that has and continues to treat Black people as less than, in many ways – how has he explored his own personal privilege whilst being underrepresented and marginalized simultaneously?

> When I'm in the professional environment, at work at Dell, doing this job, people respect me and my role and I am treated properly. But I will tell you, on a normal day before Covid, depending on how I'm dressed and where I am (where nobody knows my professional background or job), if I'm not dressed like 'the professional businessman', it becomes very, very clear that I'm the Black guy. I walk into a nice shopping mall, a high-end or boutique store and I am still treated the same as I was when I was a young Black man in South Central LA. If I walked by one of those stores back then or now, people treat you differently because of their bias towards their social stereotype.

> So this means I walk that line every day. However, I recognize I do have this privilege (like you as another person of colour) who is now financially stable and can open up opportunities for others. But I'm very, very quickly snatched right back into the world of where others are privileged and I am not – if I get pulled over by the cops, my mindset is that same kid I was when I was pulled over at 15 years old. That outcome is not going to be a normal interaction that others have the privilege to have, which is just 'give me your license and registration' and a friendly 'don't speed anymore, sir'. It's going to be a much different experience. Likewise, I have similar experiences when it comes to travel, where flight attendants will automatically try to send me to coach, even though I have a first-class ticket. And when I put them right, I smirk because I know just what has happened – and so do they. I want them to sit in that moment for a second to really think about what assumptions they've made.

So I just deal with those in my mind and recognize that I can't solve all of the world's ills at once. But the more and more of what we do will start to hopefully break down and have people realize how they're interacting with people that are different from them. Hopefully, if they're educated in these biases, they'll then maybe… just maybe question whether they should or shouldn't approach that person because of the way they look, but instead learn from them first.

Harnessing this power of privilege is a very real thing – and something we all must do. But what we also must do is in those moments when we are biased is move past wallowing in guilt and do something meaningful with the mistakes and hurt you have caused. Awareness of privilege is only one small step here. Using it for the betterment of others is the needed step:

> I want people to understand privilege is more than just feeling guilty. Privilege is simply a fact – you can do something that somebody didn't get an opportunity to do regardless of that. This isn't about whether someone gave you something or you have something that makes life easier for you. I spend time telling those people that whatever circumstance you were born in is fine. I'm not asking you to apologize for that. I'm just asking you to recognize that others didn't have that. And that you won't have people making assumptions, positively or negatively, about you (in many ways). That's a superpower and I'd like them to use it for good. Or you can use it for bad, which is to keep others out, playing a zero-sum game where you keep others from that same ability so you can assume more privilege.

> So don't think of it as it's 'I'm in a special club, and I don't want anybody else'. Think of it as if you're in a club, that you have some powers that you can get some other people into the club. Right?

Using privilege to actively participate and make things better for others is where I hope many of you are at the moment (or are moving towards). One of the reasons I wanted to write this book was to help people go on this journey, in a way that was authentic, transparent and eye-opening. Brian has clearly gone on that journey and reading his story it is important to remember how easily privilege can be taken away. It can be fickle and flimsy. In the areas we both work in our organizations, we're both senior leaders who are respected and listened to. However, outside of that, we both face some similar and different biases based on being people of colour. I want all of us to remember that. That being privileged in one environment does not mean being privileged in all. Many of the stories Brian shared with me resounded so much that I felt like I said nothing but 'yes' whilst nodding profusely for almost 10 minutes whilst he spoke. Now, we are both different age groups, different ethnicities and living in two different countries – yet we have so many similarities in our experiences. And why is that? It's because bias is baked into society, and we must now do more to challenge it in ourselves and around us.

Like I asked all of the leaders I had the privilege of interviewing, I asked Brian what would be the one piece of advice he would give to those who are aiming to demand more of their leadership? What would be the one thing he'd suggest you all do. He said:

> My one piece of advice is that if you're going to ask more of your leader, literally put the case together as to the why, what, how and why I'm asking for more, using stats on why this makes good sense to back up your thoughts. And it's not because I'm asking for more for myself personally – this is much bigger than any one of us. Root this ask in why this is better for the company and its culture overall – then those demands become less of a demand and more of a partnership. Make it clear this is a two-way street where they want your help and you want theirs – both groups working together on education, awareness, accountability and goals. Remember that we are working together on this – mistakes will be made and we must acknowledge, apologize and learn from them. Always remain curious – because those that are curious learn more than those who aren't.

Planning for more is never easy – especially in DE&I – but it is necessary. Inclusion work cannot be ad hoc and community driven, as it then gets pushed to the side when time, money or resources get tight. I couldn't sum it up better than Brian. I want all of us to remain curious, to remain engaged and inquisitive, because by actively seeking different perspectives, understandings and experiences, we can truly start and continue to create a society with workplaces that truly value all people – equally and equitably.

References

Cook, I (2015) [accessed 13 December 2020] How HR Can Tackle Diversity Using the Rooney Rule [Online] www.visier.com/clarity/how-hr-can-tackle-diversity-using-the-rooney-rule (archived at https://perma.cc/NQ3T-FYZU)

Dell, M (2020) [accessed 13 December 2020] Standing Strong Together, LinkedIn, 1 June [online] https://www.linkedin.com/pulse/standing-strong-together-michael-dell (archived at https://perma.cc/VNY7-C5LR)

Gov.UK (2011) [accessed 13 December 2020] Women on Boards, www.gov.uk [Online] https://assets.publishing.service.gov.uk/government/uploads/system/uploads/attachment_data/file/31480/11-745-women-on-boards.pdf (archived at https://perma.cc/QR9W-9SHU)

Lorenzetti, L (2015) [accessed 13 December 2020] What Pinterest is Learning from the Pittsburgh Steelers about Diversity [Online] https://fortune.com/2015/07/30/pinterest-diversity-initiative/ (archived at https://perma.cc/AY65-MESC)

Midkiff, S (2020) [accessed 13 December 2020] Jonathan Price was a 'Hometown Hero': Police Shot & Killed Him for Trying to Break up a Fight, www.refinery29.com [Online] www.refinery29.com/en-gb/2020/10/10076931/jonathan-price-police-shooting-wolfe-city-texas-murder-charge (archived at https://perma.cc/7984-UAZD)

Terjesen, S, Aguilera, RV and Lorenz, R (2014) Legislating a woman's seat on the board: Institutional factors driving gender quotas for boards of directors, *Journal of Business Ethics*, **128** (2), pp 233–51

Conclusion

Firstly, writing this book has been a phenomenal experience. I have always enjoyed writing, but I wrote this with the particular goal of providing a resource for everyone to understand diversity, equity and inclusion, from the history behind it to meaningful actionable and measurable ways for people and companies to make a significant change in this space. I wanted to write something that was quite literally for everyone – not just those who were already engaged in DE&I or who already understood all of the common terms. Because this is everyone's job. Every single one of us has a role here – we should all be angry that the world treats people so differently based on their gender identity, ethnicity, disabilities, sexual orientations, neurodiversities, ages, culture and more. And we should all harness this anger in ways that allow us to move past awareness and onto action.

I am a firm believer that we cannot tackle inclusion without education and discussions on exclusion. We did not get here by accident. I dislike the passive nature that many have taken, labelling exclusion or bias as 'unconscious', as opposed to recognizing that people have done horrible things that have brought us to this position. Through this book, I hope you have gained a better idea or awareness of the historic events that have affected those from underrepresented backgrounds – some in extremely violent ways.

This work takes time. And there is no silver bullet. We can't expect our efforts to change things overnight. I need you to bear with this, remember that not everything will be a win but that, in the long term, this will pay off. We can make real, meaningful changes here, if we persevere against the inevitable friction. Some people in high positions will disengage from this work. In October 2020, the then-sitting President of the United States, Donald Trump, signed an executive order barring federally funded entities from conducting 'divisive' forms of workplace unconscious bias training (Smith, 2020). Notably, despite Trump's well-known divisive rhetoric, with a wave of 'allyship' sweeping the globe in the wake of George Floyd's death at the hands of police brutality, white women still showed up and voted for Trump more in 2020 than in 2016 (Essence, 2020).

Please keep in mind that this is not limited to the United States. Following the order from Trump in the United States, the UK Conservative Party followed swiftly behind stating if 'any school teaches these elements of critical race theory… [it] is breaking the law' (Trilling, 2020). In September 2020, the UK government confirmed it was stopping plans to allow transgender people to 'self-ID', causing a huge hit to the LGBT+ communities (Wareham, 2020).

All of these decisions will have an effect now and they will continue to have effects much later too. I want each of us to remember that we must fight, push and challenge these types of decisions – both for people we identify with and those we do not identify with. To do this, I want you to remember:

- Diversity without inclusion is fruitless. We cannot claim to embrace diversity without actively doing the work to create inclusive environments. Reworking business and cultural norms is a necessity and one we must do by default.

- We will be wrong and we will get challenged – and that is ok. Humans are flawed by default. You are no exception. Remember that. There will be times when you think you did something good but it wasn't quite right. Accept the feedback, rework and move on. Don't put yourself at the centre – this isn't about you.
- Embed inclusion in your business and life. Where you can, capture and add a data lens to absolutely everything. Make no assumptions that what you do is inclusive – use research and data to back up these thoughts. If the data tells you something that opposes your thoughts, remember this is likely your bias, emotion and prejudice at play. Sit back and remember the point above!
- Allyship is the key to unlocking the power of diversity. All of us must be engaged, both on a personal and a systemic level, to make real change for those who have been underrepresented, underappreciated and undervalued in the industry for so long. This is a journey and is absolutely not self-defined. Keep an eye out for performative allyship, both in yourself and others, and call it out when you see it happen.
- Privilege must be part of your daily thought process. The world doesn't exist without it; therefore, neither should you. Actively consider your and other people's privilege (or lack thereof) in your decision making, who you are drawn to, who you dislike, who you decide to listen to and who you don't. Bias plays hand in hand with privilege and it's important to acknowledge this every day. This means taking more time on decision making and spending time and headspace on really thinking about why you're making a decision, who it affects and whether it affects different groups of people disproportionately.

Society, people and the world have been purposefully and deliberately exclusive in upholding the power white, non-disabled, heterosexual, financially stable people have. We must be purposefully and deliberately inclusive to create a society that no longer greatly advantages some whilst intentionally disadvantaging others. I am asking you to make sure you actively push and fight for equity and equality for all of those around you – not just those you directly identify with. We must demand more, and we must do it now.

References

Essence (2020) [accessed 13 December 2020] 55 Percent of White Women, 18 Percent of Black Men Voted for Donald Trump: Exit Poll [Online] www.essence.com/news/politics/55-percent-white-women-trump-election-2020/ (archived at https://perma.cc/V2FB-Q6QR)

Smith, P (2020) [accessed 13 December 2020] Trump Didn't Ban All Unconscious-Bias Training: DOL Official [Online] https://news.bloomberglaw.com/daily-labor-report/trump-didnt-ban-all-unconscious-bias-training-dol-official (archived at https://perma.cc/W8HF-EKQH)

Trilling, D (2020) [accessed 13 December 2020] Why is the UK Government Suddenly Targeting 'Critical Race Theory'? *The Guardian*, 23 October [Online] www.theguardian.com/commentisfree/2020/oct/23/uk-critical-race-theory-trump-conservatives-structural-inequality (archived at https://perma.cc/FL5R-2FZE)

Wareham, J (2020) [accessed 13 December 2020] U.K. Drops Trans Rights Self-ID Reform of Gender Recognition Act in Major Blow to LGBTQ Rights, *Forbes* [Online] www.forbes.com/sites/jamiewareham/2020/09/22/uk-scraps-transgender-reforms-in-major-blow-to-lgbtq-rights--but-will-open-three-new-gics/#53fbe63a12d3 (archived at https://perma.cc/XR7Q-ZPZL)

Index

CPSIA information can be obtained
at www.ICGtesting.com
Printed in the USA
BVHW020158280321
603527BV00017B/97

9 781398 600447